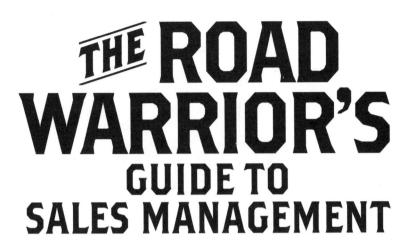

THE ROAD WARRIOR'S
GUIDE TO
SALES MANAGEMENT

Taking the Stress Out of Managing Salespeople

by Tom Schaber

Adams Business & Professional

Edina, Minnesota

ISBN 10: 1-59298-199-2
ISBN 13: 978-1-59298-199-1

Library of Congress Control Number: 2007937990
Printed in the United States of America
First Printing: January 2008
12 11 10 09 08   6 5 4 3 2 1

Cover and interior design by Clay Schotzko

Adams Business & Professional

Adams Business & Professional is an imprint of
Beaver's Pond Press, Inc.
7104 Ohms Lane
Edina, MN 55439-2129
(952) 829-8818
www.BeaversPondPress.com

To order, visit www.BookHouseFulfillment.com
or call 1-800-901-3480. Reseller discounts available.

THE ROAD
WARRIOR'S
GUIDE TO
SALES MANAGEMENT

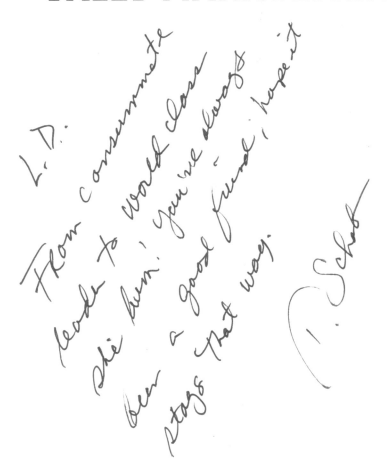

L.D.

From consummate
leader to World Class
the best. You've always
been a good friend. I hope it
stays that way.

T. Schod

This book is dedicated to my wife, Cathy, who gave me the opportunity to chase some dreams while traveling the country for the better part of fifteen years. I left town each week, comfortable with the knowledge that she could handle any situation that popped up with the house or kids. That's not to say that there weren't times when she gritted her teeth, thinking that maybe there was another job in Minneapolis I might like. The adage "behind every good man is a good woman" is spot-on correct! We've managed to come through the traveling and other challenges with a love that's going on thirty-eight years. I love you Cassy.

The book is also dedicated to our kids, Pat and Sara. There were many, many weeks when my traveling got to them. They were and are phenomenal people, and I truly could not have succeeded without their patience.

Contents

Introduction

Welcome to the world of a sales manager road warrior! During the last thirty-plus years I've frequented five-star hotels and one-star motels. I've eaten exquisite cuisine as well as gut bombs on the run through airports. I've witnessed great hires and awful hires, seen great managers and not-so-hot managers. I've had 4:30 a.m. wake-up calls, have missed flights, and have gotten wedged between the gargantuan twins in the middle seat. I've suffered one-hundred-five-degree heat and bone-numbing cold. I've been part of spectacular sales meetings in Kauai and have wasted my time in Kansas City. Through all the good, the bad, and the ugly I learned a lot of lessons, forgot some, and relearned others. Most, if not all of them, are contained in the book. I hope you enjoy reading it as much as I enjoyed writing it!

How to Read the Book:
There is always adopting the good old-fashioned cover-to-cover method.

You could also read the book by chapter for specific content. The following descriptions direct you to specific parts of the book if you prefer this second strategy. Here's exactly what you'll find:

1. **The Sales Myth:** Some mistaken ideas about salespeople. Even if you've got a sales organization you might find this amusing.

2. **When to Hire a Salesperson:** Some general rules of thumb about the size of an organization, its products, and their markets that can dictate when to hire salespeople.

3. **Hiring:** Ideas about where to find salespeople and some dos and don'ts about the hiring process.

4. **Hiring—Gender and Age Questions:** Some thoughts about how age can determine rep quality. Is there a difference between male and female sales reps?

5. **Interviewing:** Covers tips on interviewing, questions to ask a sales candidate, and questions that a good rep should ask an owner or sales manager.

6. **You've Got the Right Salesperson—Now What?** Touches on the specific items to cover with a new rep once he or she is on board.

7. **Should You Assume That the Salesperson Has a Sales Process?** Touches on sales training and the value in learning a repeatable sales process.

8. **Sales Meetings:** Covers how often to have meetings, what to do in them, how long they should last, and questions the owner/manager should ask the salespeople during the meeting.

9. **Creating Goals for Salespeople:** Touches on why salespeople need goals, the steps to creating goals, the sales activities a salesperson should perform daily, and the relationship of these activities to the goals.

10. **Creating Sales Territories:** Covers how to create territories, factors that affect the creation of territories, and when to split a territory (making two from one).

11. **Getting Rid of a Sales Rep:** Covers when to let a salesperson go and the steps involved in executing the process.

12. **What the Owner as Sales Manager Should Do When Working With a Salesperson in the Field.** Covers what to do and not to do when working with a salesperson in the field.

13. **Compensation:** Covers some general guidelines for setting up a comp plan.

14. **The "Touchy-Feely" Part of Sales Management:** Covers ways to build trust with salespeople, how to encourage salespeople to develop strong loyalty to you, and how to mentally and emotionally connect with your salespeople.

15. **Wrap-Up:** Expresses thanks to several mentors and friends and offers a few parting bits of wisdom.

General Comments on Small Businesses, Their Owners, and Sales:

Managing salespeople and the process of sales seems easy if you're looking from the outside in. After all, the company you own has a product or service, you know there is a market for it, you feel that the product is high quality, and your current customers tell you the product and service are awesome. You may even have one or more salespeople to take some of the selling burden from you. As a sage once said:

You have the right product at the right time in the right market!

The sage failed to say that you may be missing one or two ingredients needed to grow your business. You may:

- Be missing salespeople to increase the rate of growth.

- Have salespeople but not the *right* ones.

- Not have the experience to manage the salespeople effectively.

With these ingredients added, the sage's advice reads:

You have the right product at the right time selling into the right market with the right people!

Selling effectiveness is one of business's forgotten step-children. It amazes me that so few business owners (and sales managers) don't appreciate the obvious fact that, until the right sales department is in place, the engine of business does not run effectively. A company can have absolutely the coolest product in the world, but until someone delivers the message about that product to people who need it, growth stands still. You may have a salesperson or salespeople, but this alone does not guarantee that the right message is being delivered in the right way to the right people.

Why do so many business owners forget this simple fact? Owners may be so busy working through their entrepreneurial dreams that they never think about how continued growth depends on effective sales. A young company may have manufacturing abilities, possibly an engineering function, and maybe some marketing. But these can fall short. At some point in a company's evolution, however, an owner will have to separate the sales function from marketing and build a sales department. So too will a sales manager have to build a sales team.

The organizational chart for a company providing a service will have no manufacturing or engineering components, but it will have marketing. And many service companies think that simple marketing will supply the magic sales bullet. A little advertising, a few speeches in the local community, a good PR firm, and bingo—sales appear. There is nothing wrong with holding any of these beliefs as long as they're supported by *a sales department that has the mission of growing the business through repeated contact with prospects and customers.*

However, having a marketing plan and a sales department is only half of the sales equation. Let's say that you're an enlightened owner/entrepreneur, that somewhere along your path to starting the business a smart mentor, professor, or some other peer told you that entrepreneurs make lousy salespeople, and that you needed to hire someone who could sell. (Don't get ruffled over the word "lousy." Entrepreneurs can often sell in the early product adoption phase but most do not have the skill to sell after that phase. And there is nothing wrong with that. Every individual plays to their strength.) And that you did. In fact, there's your sales rep over in one of the cubes toiling away at God knows what!

You, the enlightened business owner, hired a sales rep, but:

- How do you know if he or she is the right one?

- How do you know if he or she can sell?

- Do you have a sense for what you need to do to manage the sales activities of this person?

These three questions simply scratch the surface of the sales dilemma.

With all of this in mind, it made sense to me to lend a little wisdom, experience-based, to all you owners and sales managers who wonder why sales aren't happening at the rate you want and expected. This book is meant to help you manage salespeople and the sales process. You will also find information that will help you hire the right sales manager if you don't already have one. I am confident that the information in the book is accurate and practical. I'm so confident of the material that if the sales manager you hire doesn't practice the philosophy here, you should send them on his or her way because this person isn't the right one for you or your salespeople.

Why So Many Lists in the Book?
I despise reading books with countless pages of text with chapters as the only breaks. Also, fifty percent of people process information visually, so it's easier to process information

from bullet points or numbers. Lastly, lists appeal to the majority of people regardless of their personal style.

Now, you may be wondering why you should believe me. I have had thirty-plus years of successful sales and sales management experience. I've been a salesperson, sales manager, and business owner. And the thirty years were not spent selling or managing in exactly the same way. I've made a lot of mistakes and learned a great deal along the way. Also, most people like to learn from anecdotal experiences, so you'll appreciate learning about many of the experiences that impacted me. In most cases the stories will denote the differences between sales/management success and failures.

Two more items and we'll get on with it. One, most people like my direct style which uses humor and liberal amounts of sarcasm. You may not, so I apologize up front. Suffer through your occasional outbursts of emotion and frustration and pick up the messages.

Two, this book is general in nature. There have been hundreds of books written on most of the topics you'll read here. The concepts you'll learn are not meant to pass inspection by an HR specialist, a compensation plan guru, or a world-class sales trainer. The book will provide direction for a business owner and/or a sales manager when he or she is ready to hire and manage salespeople. Many owners/sales managers are not ready, based on many of the situations I have experienced. Use this book as a guide that will help you hire and build a sales organization.

Chapter One

The Sales Myth

"Mama didn't raise you to be no salesperson!"

—Unknown

If that's not from some country-western song, it should be. Tell me there's not a whole lot of truth here. When you were about six years old your mother or father probably read you a story every night and I will guarantee that the book's main character was never a sales guy. Our parents did not raise us to be salespeople! No way! At six, your parents started talking to you about what you might be when you grew up, and the answers didn't vary much from child to child; the dream was of a doctor, lawyer, nurse, or fireman. (Again, not a whisper about sales!)

Sales was not and still is not considered a profession. Ingrained and burned into our brain is the image of a slick car sales guy from the sixties. (My apologies to the professional car salespeople.) You know the guy with checkered pants, wide tie, slicked-backed hair, a bit of a paunch, and a smile that says, "here comes another sucker."

Do you remember the sitcom from the seventies called *WKRP in Cincinnati*? The sales guy was Herb and the producers of the show hardly glamorized Herb. I still get chills thinking about him! Or how about Willy Loman in *Death of a Salesman*? And in another fictional example, actor Alec Baldwin played a sales manager to a sorry group of high-pressure shmucks selling house siding. The personalities in these examples range from simpleton to huckster, with all manner of variations in between.

Now that you've got the sales guy stereotype planted in your mind, let me blow it out of the water.

Sales is a profession!

Don't flip to the next chapter. Don't shake your head. Don't think that just because I'm a sales guy of course I will proclaim sales to be a profession. I've sold, managed salespeople, hired and fired salespeople, and trained salespeople for the last thirty years. I've been in front of thousands of customers, closed business, lost business, carried a detail bag, and entertained some world-famous cardiologists, people who I call good friends. (Believe me, they would not have bought from me *or* even dealt with me if they didn't think I was a professional.)

So let's shift this little paradigm here. Sales is a profession. Period. There is a science to selling just as there is a science and process to what most of us consider professions: physician, lawyer, engineer, etc. But not all people believe this, particularly many business owners who believe that if you do a good pitch to the customer, they'll buy. They often ask "Who needs a sales guy anyway? They're a dime a dozen!" Well, you would be right, there are a large group of salespeople who are a dime a dozen but there is another smaller group of salespeople who embody professionalism when they meet with customers and prospects. Let's see why they are different.

Successful sales professionals share these traits:

- They dress and look like professionals and have the right clothes, haircuts, shined shoes, etc. **They respect themselves and expect respect from others!**

- When asked about their goals they will describe, clearly, both their personal and business goals. **They know exactly where they're going and how much money they will earn.**

- They will be working at specific sales activities at any time of the day. **They are focused!**

- They communicate effectively and know how to listen. **In fact, they listen more than they talk!**

- They are organized. **Professional salespeople do not like leaving anything to chance!**

- They provide phenomenal customer service, to the point that their customers are willing to pay more for products they sell. **Professional salespeople sell product *value!***

- Most sales professionals have excellent leadership skills. **Other salespeople will come to them for advice and mentoring!**

- They always make their sales revenue goals. **They follow a sales plan!**

- They are motivated by money and recognition. **They are competitive!**

- They follow an organized sales process. **Their sales presentations are systematic!**

At best this is a partial listing, but you get a sense of the characteristics these professional salespeople possess.

Even though sales is a profession, not all salespeople are professionals. You thought this was going to be easy, right? Visualize a bell curve and think of the area to the far right. At this part of the curve you have the top ten percent of all salespeople, the true sales professionals. Of course, you're asking where this number comes from. During thirty years working in sales organizations I looked at the people I worked for, the peers I worked with, and those who I managed. The number of people in those three groups is in the high hundreds. The percentages indicate that out of these people no more than ten percent were sales professionals as defined above. Based on my experiences and the experience of other managers I have consulted the percentage is realistic.

No bell curve describing the success patterns of salespeople is complete without describing other types of salespeople. If the top ten percent represent sales professionals then the ten percent at the other end of the bell curve are the bottom feeders. They are the polar opposites of the people described above. Looking at this group you'll find that some or all of the following are true of them:

- Their résumés read like fables. **You'll find gaps in their employment!**

- They do not have well-articulated or written goals. **Chances are they have no goals!**

- Their cars look like trash and they look disheveled. **They make lousy first impressions!**

- They don't appear "together." **They leave the sample that they should have had on the sales call in the office; they have no customer records so they don't remember the names of their contacts; and they ramble on about the features of their product.**

- They make poor eye contact. **They don't observe the prospect!**

- They talk about features and benefits rather than listen to a prospect's needs. **They think that by talking they have control of the sales call!**

- Reaching their revenue goals is due more to luck than executing a sales plan. **They don't realize that luck has nothing to do with achieving revenue goals!**

- With luck these salespeople may put in 3-4 hours of actual sales-related work during any given day. **Their time management is non-existent!**

Between these two extremes you have the remaining eighty percent of the salespeople. Those salespeople in the 70th to 90th percentile have a good chance of moving into the top ten. They're not missing that much; a good sales coach will help these folks move up easily. The sales reps in the 10th to 30th percentile are the weakest reps; they have moments when they surprise people, but generally they do as little as possible and don't leave very positive vibes with others around them.

The remaining forty percent can go either way, literally. These are also the people that deserve more time from the owner/manager. Thinking back to my time as a sales manager, I see that I spent roughly half my time in the field with those reps in the middle of the bell curve and another thirty percent with the top ten percent. Spending more than twenty percent of one's time with the remainder of the salespeople is hardly worth the effort. Many managers, including me, feel that they can turn these salespeople around, but the chances of this happening are between slim and none. In essence you beat yourself up thinking that it's your job to rescue people from Dante's sales hell! Believe me, there are not enough antacid preparations around to get you through that mess.

Chapter Two

When Will You Need to Hire a Salesperson?

"The more important question to ask is will you be able to deal with the increase in sales"?

—Unknown

There may be hard and fast rules or a formula for when to hire, but I'm not sure what they are. I can, however, share several situations I experienced, as an employee and consultant, that may shed some light on the decision.

In 1982 a company that barely did $8M in annual revenue selling a cardiovascular device hired five direct field salespeople. Initially, the company had distributed the product through independent reps who didn't fully understand the procedure or the technology. Though it's common practice for small companies to market products in this way, it does not work in all situations and it didn't work for this company. After that experiment failed, the direct salespeople (5) were hired to cover the country and sell the device. The procedure for which the device was designed was called coronary angioplasty and it was the hottest topic in the medical community. A salesperson could walk into the hospital and practically get orders for the product in the lobby. Given the hot marketplace and the high quality of the product, the timing was perfect to bring on direct reps.

I once consulted with a company in Minneapolis that sold packaging supplies. The owner, who also was the main salesperson and a real sales pro—probably the best I've ever seen, had bought the company from the original owner. After building the business to around $2M in sales, he hired his first salesperson. The owner needed to hire additional reps because he couldn't grow the business fast enough while simultaneously selling and running the business. The company, a regional rather than national company, is now around $10M with five salespeople including the owner. I like the idea that the owner maintains contact with a select group of customers.

Another $8M company with which I consulted had one main salesperson, the owner, as well as several regional distributors. The company is just now hiring their first direct rep, mainly due to new product introductions. Why add a salesperson now? The timing is right to put more "feet on the street" in order to get the new product message out to people more quickly. Should there be more than one direct rep? Ideally, yes, but the company manufacturing the product has some short-term production limitations. Having too many salespeople could put the company into backorder on the product. Not good!

Are there any hard and fast rules for when to hire? Here are several general scenarios that might shed some light on possible answers.

Company A has revenue in the 0-$500K range. This company has one consultant or owner who may have spun off from a corporate environment and bought the company/technology or created the product. The company has been around for at least a year.

- The product is intangible or tangible.

- The market for the product is competitive or not, depending on a host of factors.

- The company's new customers come from advertising, direct mail, networking, referrals, associations, cold calling, competitors, and personal contacts in the marketplace, or any combination of these.

- The consultant/owner is technically sophisticated (he or she knows their product) but selling is not his or her forte. For all intents and purposes the owner is not good at selling but has been successful plucking "the low-hanging fruit" from a new technology or new product. The next round of customers will present greater selling challenges.

- The consultant closes from 10-20 percent of the prospects he/she has seen.

- If the company survives past its first year and the business grows moderately, the consultant/owner is overwhelmed because he or she is juggling too many business responsibilities.

- The product is not proprietary but it could have some "wrinkles" in it that the present customers like and that distinguish it from similar products.

If I were the owner of Company A, I would be tempted to hire a sales rep even though it might be a tad risky. However, the following conditions would have to exist before I hired.

- Demand for the product is solid.

- The technology is relatively easy for the sales-person to learn and understand.

- The sales cycle is relatively short, several weeks to a month tops.

- The salesperson will be willing to embrace risk since the failure rate for start-up or small companies are extremely high. In this scenario the salesperson will have a low base salary with the majority of the income coming from commissions.

- The product is not generic.

- The margins are reasonably high, in the twenty percent or above range.

- Cash flow is sufficient for the owner to pay commissions.

Company B has revenue in the $500K-$2M range. It has been in existence for several years.

- Product is intangible or tangible.

- Market is probably competitive.

- One or several owners are primarily responsible for business development but also have responsibility for running the business.

- Some current revenue comes from existing clients. New business comes from networking, participation in associations, talks, referrals, and prospecting. Owners may want to grow the business but may not be comfortable with a more proactive sales effort. Typically these types of owners are technically sophisticated but not sales sophisticated.

- Business could be slowing or stagnant. The majority of business comes from current customers.

- The owner(s) experimented with hiring a salesperson but the results were poor and they've hired and fired several reps. The company may have one or two inside salespeople who make outbound cold calls. It's possible that this organization also has an outside salesperson. The owners sell but not as much as they did when the company started.

- The company seems to have hit a wall, i.e., growth is minimal. The owners hope they don't lose any current clients.

This is a classic situation and one I believe exists for many, many companies.

The two million dollar mark is one of the larger-than-life road bumps that sink companies or forever doom them to two million dollars. Why? In part because the owners are too naïve or stubborn to get serious about hiring the *right* salespeople. This type of company experiences sales rep turnover because the owners hire any person as long as he or she fogs a mirror. The other obstacle is that the owners are spread too thin. They are forced to run the business, meet with the banker, meet with the HR consultant, bring on new products, settle differences, figure out the newest software, sell, and ... well, you get the idea. And if the owner is the founder/engineer of the company, they will often be stubborn about relinquishing control of sales.

If I were the owner of Company B I'd hire a sales rep immediately. In fact, this company is in dire need of hiring a salesperson, maybe two. The following conditions probably exist and would warrant hiring:

- The product is well received by current customers.

- There are a significant number of prospects who should see the product but the owners can't get to them or they don't know *how* to get to them.

- The owners have other responsibilities piling up and they cannot spend enough time selling.

- The inside salesperson can generate leads and may close some business but the majority of "closes" need to be done in person.

- There is competition but it's not overwhelming.

- Revenue has fluctuated between $1.5M and $2M over the last several years but the rate of growth is slowing.

- The company currently has an edge, but more competitors, in addition to the existing ones, are on the horizon.

- The owners have exhausted the easy sales, that is, the low-hanging fruit, but they are not doing well with the more difficult sales situations.

Company C has revenue in the $2M to $8M range. This company has been in existence anywhere from several years to over ten.

- The owners have some responsibility for business development but find it extremely difficult to balance all responsibilities.

- Growth is meeting projections but the owners want to accelerate the process.

- There are one or more salespeople but the owner wants to hire more to stimulate additional growth. The owners don't manage the salespeople; they assume the reps are organized and know what they are doing.

- Growth spikes after new salespeople are hired, then levels off. The owners wonder why this happens so they put pressure on the salespeople to hit the numbers and sell more. Salespeople are frustrated because the owners really don't know that much about coaching or motivating salespeople.

- The sales department is fairly well defined in terms of personnel, although it does not necessarily have an identity as yet. Identity to me is that the sales department is considered separate from marketing; the salespeople are known for strong product knowledge, aggressive prospecting, and better-than-average selling techniques, something that separates them from average salespeople.

- The sales process, if there is one, is OK but still not that well defined.

- Database software may be in use, but it is not being used effectively.

- Sales meetings are infrequent, when they happen at all.

If I were the owner of Company C, I'd reassess my salespeople. This company is in need of hiring better salespeople, adding to or perhaps replacing the existing ones. The following conditions probably exist and would warrant hiring:

- The potential for the product is significant and is currently marketed to companies in one vertical market. The product may have applications in other markets.

- The owners are transitioning out of sales completely, which means that existing salespeople or the new ones will have to take over the owner's accounts.

- The sales cycle is not long and the ratio of closes to appointments is fairly high.

- If the existing reps are doing well, they find it difficult adding more business because of the time it takes to service or stay in contact with their current customers.

- The company may be adding or developing new products.

- The company is poised to grow quickly.

- The company has a window where they might become a serious player in the marketplace.

I run into these situations consistently. The decision has been made to hire more salespeople but no one, particularly the owner(s), knows what the optimum number of salespeople should be or what to do with the new reps once they are hired. Frankly, having or identifying the ideal number of salespeople is less important than managing the ones that are already there!

Once a company generates revenue in the $6M to $10M range, they enter the "should-I-hire-or-should-I-not-hire" a sales manager quandary. There are so many variables surrounding this decision that it's practically impossible to document them all. Are the reps local or remote? Are the reps seasoned veterans or is there a mix of veterans and rookies? Are the reps order-takers or do they actually have to sell? Does the owner know how to manage salespeople and/or does he or she have the time to do that job effectively?

In a situation like the one just described, I would have an independent source evaluate the sales organization to determine whether they need to be managed. A good consultant can ride along with a sales rep and know within a day or two of sales calls whether the person is a pro, a semi-pro, or a world-class dud. The chances are better than average that most sales groups have a combination of good salespeople, average ones, and those who should not be in sales. Given these conditions—a mix of different skill levels—I would hire a sales manager to reform the ranks and hire true pros.

Finally, here is the real rub. I made a comment earlier that about ten percent of all salespeople are real pros, which leaves ninety percent that are fairly good, average, or bad. The ninety percent group will absolutely need some direction. Typically, these reps do not follow a sales process; their goals are murky, if they exist at all; and more than likely, their territory management is weak. In these situations a good sales manager is warranted.

Let's look at one more company where hiring is an issue.

Company D has revenue of $10M plus. This company has been in existence for a minimum of five years out to ten to twelve years.

- Typically, this company already has several outside salespeople. The salespeople may or may not have a dedicated sales manager and so might still be managed by the owner of the company. There may be a sales process or system to selling, but it may not be practiced by all the reps consistently.

- The salespeople vary in age and they have had no professional sales development or coaching. The sales culture is chaotic, the salespeople do not have well-documented sales plans, and accountability is poor. The owner is frustrated because sales are below expectations and the pipeline remains full of unclosed business.

- Weekly sales meetings are pressure-filled because the president/owner wants more sales but doesn't offer a clear sales strategy or process.

- The owner hires additional salespeople, assuming that increased numbers will increase sales.

- If there are more than three or four salespeople, the owner may promote one of the salespeople to sales manager. The owner thinks that since he or she has off-loaded the responsibility of managing the salespeople, the problem of poor sales will resolve itself. The owner assumes that the salespeople will react better if managed by one of their own.

- The sales department takes on an identity. *Again, the word "identity" is vague. But, typically, sales teams do create a style or distinct approach to how they do business. They're good at prospecting, they give phenomenal customer service, or they're great closers. Sales teams create their own identities. I believe that sales teams should be assembled based on what the owner wants or what the industry dictates.*

If I were the owner of Company D, I'd recognize my mistake and hire an experienced sales manager. This is the last scenario and one of the scariest, primarily because of the second-to-last bullet point. Companies promote one salesperson to the position of sales manager more often than not because doing so is convenient; usually one of the salespeople is head and shoulders above the rest and therefore is dubbed manager. Also, the owner may be sick to death of managing a bunch of stubborn salespeople and wants out of that responsibility.

Let's imagine that the rep who was promoted was a hunter, which in sales terminology means someone who loves to prospect for new business and is good at it. Four bad things then occur: 1) The hunter becomes frustrated because he is out of his comfort zone in the sales management role. 2) He wants to reincarnate all the salespeople into reps with his selling style. This won't work because salespeople have their own style. 3) Sales decrease because new business from the hunter falls off. 4) The hunter-turned-sales manager maintains a sales territory in addition to managing the other reps, and gets overwhelmed and overworked. *Do not under any circumstances hire a sales manager and give him or her responsibility for his or her own accounts. This person's number one responsibility is to work with the salespeople to develop their selling skills!* I'll say more about this.

Some General Rules of Thumb on Choosing Sales Managers:

- **Your best salesperson will seldom make the best sales manager.** Sales managers are wired differently than are salespeople. (More on this later.) Your best salesperson is the best at what he or she does for a reason—he or she likes to prospect and close business. This person is money-motivated and coaching others is probably not one of their strong suits.

- **Your sales manager should manage the salespeople and that's it!** This is really non-negotiable, although there are differing opinions on this. You may need to accept this on faith. Managing and having responsibility for a sales territory (or just key accounts) *is* mutually exclusive. The job the sales manager has is to develop the skills of the salespeople, to mentor and coach them, and to hold them accountable for their sales behaviors. That, my friend, is a full-time job.

- **You'll need to use an assessment tool to identify the right candidate to lead your salespeople.** If you use such a tool to identify the right salespeople, as you'll see in the next chapter, why not use one to choose the right manager? The skills that great salespeople have are often different than those of a good manager. Developing salespeople is a black art. Very few organizations teach sales management, so a manager seldom has a road map going into the job. The good ones have an innate feel for what it takes to coach and mentor other people.

- **Your sales manager needs to be able to do his or her job.** You run the company; let the sales manager run the salespeople. The more you look over his or her shoulder, the less creative he or she will be; the manager will tend to want to please you, and this might mean not doing what's right by the salespeople.

- **A sales manager should have had experience selling.** I know; this sounds stupid but I have seen a sales VP put a marketing manager into a sales manager position. If you've never sold, how can you build salespeople's skills? The answer is pretty obvious: you can't.

- **Ideally, your sales manager should be familiar with the company's industry.** Will a sales manager from outside the industry fail? Not necessarily. Learning a new industry and new salespeople seems to be a daunting task. It's not impossible and I am sure that people have done it. It just seems easier to bring in an individual who is familiar with the industry.

- **Your comp plan for a manager should include a base salary plus a percentage of what the reps generate in sales.** Sales managers are driven by money, the same as salespeople. Can you imagine how frustrating it would be for a sales manager to dramatically improve the skills of the salespeople, resulting in significant growth, and then not share in the increased sales commissions? Don't even think about keeping the sales manager on a straight salary!

Chapter Three

Hiring

"If you think hiring professionals is expensive, try hiring amateurs."

—Unknown

So many owners ask the age-old question: how do I know if I've hired the right person? The short answer and the absolute truth is, you don't! And you won't until you see this person generate sales.

However, you can do some things that increase the odds of hiring the right person to sell your company's product. The following represent several legitimate courses of action you can pursue to ensure that you are hiring the right person for your company:

- **Never believe a résumé**. There are so many creative ways to cover up poor performance, gaps in employment, and reasons for short-term employment. The average person who is hiring is left with very little concrete information on which to base a decision. If you're confused by a resume, it is your right to dig for specific information about where this individual has worked and for how long. *Do not shy away from being direct in your questioning!*

Always ask the person for the contact information of his or her former sales manager. Call this person and get feedback from them directly. Ultimately, you have to ask the former manager *if he or she would hire this person again; yes or no?* If he or she pauses for even the briefest moment, you know that the person is trying to find an answer that is acceptable to you and that doesn't cast a negative light on the salesperson.

Several years ago I received a call from the owner of a company who was interviewing a salesperson who had left our company several months before. Of course, the gentleman asked pretty typical questions and I tried extremely hard to make it sound like the salesperson in question would be a good hire. The owner and I kept lobbing vague questions and equally vague answers back and forth until he asked the ultimate can't-back-out-of-a-direct-answer question. He asked, "Would you hire this person back if you had the chance, yes or no?" I could tell by his voice that he did not want a vanilla answer, so I told him no! He said thanks and hung up.

- This is a reasonable question to ask. Again, if you ever use this question, pay close attention to *how fast the person responds*. If there is any hesitancy in the response, you know that the individual means no (I would not hire the person back) regardless of what he or she says.

- When you follow up on references you can call the Human Resource department of the salesperson's previous company. Bear in mind that the only information HR is required to give you is the dates of the salesperson's employment. There is another strategy that will give you more information. Locate one of the other salespeople, marketing people, or customer service reps in the candidate's former company. Ask them for feedback on the person you are interviewing. You can also ask for references and/or call former customers. You will get accurate information from these sources. (But question references. Who would put down a bad reference? No one; stick with the people who will give you the best feedback, namely customers and other individuals in the candidate's past company. You can call references but I believe you should have very specific questions for the references. If you don't have specific questions that pertain to specific issues, then the information you receive will be meaningless.)

- **Ask prospective salespeople to bring with them reports detailing their last several years' performance**. The good reps sometimes have these; the poor to bad ones never seem to have them. Should you eliminate a rep because he or she doesn't have this? No. Will you find an exceptional rep that doesn't carry them around? Yes. Regardless, it's nice to see proof of prior performance, but it is not mandatory.

- **Hire an individual with prior selling experience.** Now this might sound obvious but I have seen owners hire a salesperson based on the fact that he is a friend of someone the owner knows or is a friend of one of the salespeople in the company. Avoid hiring acquaintances of your existing salespeople unless you know the candidate has been successful and he or she tests as successful.

- Also, don't make charity hires. Someone in your organization who knows a person looking for a sales position might say, "I'd like to have you consider Bob; he's really a good guy but just hasn't found the right job. I think he'd fit in perfectly here and I think he's a natural for sales." **If the individual has had no experience in sales do not hire him or her—period.** You don't learn sales by reading a book or going to a seminar. Professional salespeople learn their craft over time and through experience. Would you see a doctor who isn't board certified? Would you hire a lawyer who hasn't taken the boards or who has no experience? Ergo, you should not hire a salesperson who does not have some prior sales experience.

- **If possible hire an individual with experience in your industry or at least some experience in a related industry.** I've paid for my hiring blunders in very large ways. I once hired an individual who sold some very low-tech medical supplies to sell some fairly sophisticated medical devices. Intellectually he understood the product but he couldn't talk with physicians without breaking out in a ferocious sweat. Working with him was, at times, painful because I could see he was very uncomfortable. A business associate who knew this person had referred him to me. He looked good in the suit, had good communication skills, and handled himself professionally, but in the end it was a bad charity hire. Ooooops!

- Time is your greatest enemy if you hire someone with no industry experience. You want a salesperson at least up and running "on the street" within a minimum of a few weeks to six weeks, more or less depending on the complexity of the product. Four to six weeks means the sales rep is on the street selling. It does not mean that the rep is productive, i.e., generating sales. The general rule of thumb is that it takes at least six months for a rep to learn the product, the industry, and the customers. Along about the sixth month the rep becomes comfortable and starts to be productive, i.e., closing business. (Please understand that these are broad time frames. Your industry, product complexity, etc. change the dynamics.)

- There is a conundrum in the whole hiring process. Do you hire a person with experience in the industry or do you hire the best salesperson regardless of industry experience? If someone pinned me down on this I would suggest hiring the best salesperson regardless of industry experience. Here's the way my twisted logic runs. If you hire a sales professional, he or she will instinctively know what must be done to get up to speed in a new job and/or industry. Such people are hard-wired to understand what they have to do. After all, there is no guarantee that a salesperson with industry experience will do any better after the first six months with the company than the person with no such experience. This will always be one of those hiring dilemmas. Here's the bottom line. If you have two sales professionals, one with experience in the industry and one without the experience, hire the one with the experience. If you have two sales reps, one who is a true sales professional and one who is not a professional but who has experience, hire the professional sales rep.

- **Use a testing component before you hire a sales rep.** There are many good assessment tools on the market. The two that I've used are the DISC profile and the Preview offered by Profiles International. If you have HR consultants, have them help you choose a system. Such tools give you another way to evaluate a person besides depending on your gut instinct, which seven times out of ten will fail. The interview, the résumé, and an assessment tool are the three legs of the hiring stool. Use all three and save yourself some sleepless nights.

- **Have another person, in addition to you, interview the candidate.** Once owners/managers decide to hire a sales rep, they often rush ahead to get it done. Here is the catch-22. You want so badly to hire a rep that you get too emotionally involved and overlook obvious flaws. You've waited this long, so why rush the process? One way to slow things down is to involve other interviewers.

  I've actually heard owners say: he's not the perfect candidate but I need someone now. Oh, great! You hire a sales amateur, throw them out on the street, and in six months you're back looking for another salesperson. Your sense of urgency or panic led you to hire the wrong person. If you have an HR consultant, have that person interview the rep. If one is not available, use another company owner you may know or even a friend who knows your business or have a savvy person within your company interview this individual. The third-party feedback will provide a good check and balance when making too quick a hiring decision.

- **Have the candidate sell you a product during the interview.** OK, this is cruel! Hiring the right person is a key decision, so why not see if this person understands the mechanics of selling! *Here's an anecdote from my early career that very much proves this point. During the very first sales job I ever interviewed for, I was asked to sell a Styrofoam cup to the interviewer. WHAT? I* *did not know the first thing about what I was supposed to do. My performance was comic and awful. I stammered, never asked questions, made lousy eye contact, and never listened. Basically, I talked about how great the cup was. Sure, and that's going to convince someone to buy! All in all it was a miserable performance. Looking back on it, I recall the two people interviewing me were veterans of the hiring wars. They knew what they wanted and at the time it wasn't me. They could not afford to hire a rookie.* I vowed that if I ever became a manager I'd never use the same technique. Why? I thought this brought too much negative pressure on a new rep, but I was wrong. The pressure is good for both parties. I now do this routinely at companies where I consult. Many years later I bumped into the same person who did the 'Styrofoam cup' interview on me. We discussed what to me was a terrifying experience. He said that the company he worked for could not risk hiring someone without sales experience. He and his partner felt that an impromptu selling exercise was the best way to weed out inexperienced reps.

- *Another comic experience occurred not long after the Styrofoam cup incident. I interviewed with a well-known insurance company that put me through extensive pre-hire testing. The results indicated that I didn't have the ideal personality or style to be an insurance salesperson. It was a bad year for interviewing, but in hindsight it was a great year for*

*not taking the wrong job, both from my perspective
and the perspective of the employers.*

- There is value in having a sales candidate sell you something during the interview. You can assess the following. Does the rep ask questions about your needs? Does he or she talk non-stop about features and benefits in an attempt to close you? Is the candidate so nervous he or she can't form sentences? Does this salesperson have a structured process to the way he or she sells? Does the person know how to handle objections if you give them some? Is he or she mentally organized? You, as owner or manager, have a right to do anything within reason to ensure candidates can sell. After all, your company depends on it. Put them on the spot!

- I would add this comment. Prior to asking a sales candidate to role play, create a scenario that makes sense and write it down so the person can read it and have a better idea of what he or she should do. And give the person a few minutes to put some thoughts together.

- **Never talk to just one candidate no matter how good she or he looks.** I'd suggest evaluating at least three to five people. Test each one using the assessment tool. If you interview just one person you'll create reasons to hire him or her; if you interview more than five people you'll take forever to make a decision. One wise man I consulted for advice asked me what you should do if you don't find the right person after the fifth person's interview. Obviously, keep interviewing! If you're fortunate to find the right person before you've got to five people, consider yourself lucky. Hire the person, but make sure you've interviewed a few others.

Two questions many business owners and sales managers ask are, "Where do I find good salespeople?" and "Should I use a recruiter/head hunter?" The answers are anywhere, and no.

Okay, there is a little tongue-in-cheek in the answer on whether to use recruiters. There are reputable recruiters as well as your basic duds, just as in any profession. If you have a reputable recruiter and you don't mind paying the fees, then use him or her. It is time-consuming to look for reps, so using a recruiter will save time and frustration.

One of my first business mentors told me after I was promoted to sales management that I couldn't use a recruiter to fill a sales position. **What?** There was no negotiating. He told me to find them on my own! At the time I had one very big disadvantage: my network was extremely limited. So naturally I didn't have a wealth of people to tap into for names of candidates. As a result here's what happened:

I found a gentleman who seemed to fit the bill. At the time I was working for a medical company and this gentleman had experience in the industry. I told him the absolute truth about the job. The company was small so there was risk, but there would also be significant financial rewards if the company prospered; the territory required four days per week of travel over a ten state area—all by air. I told him to talk to his wife and make sure that she would be on board with the decision. I said: Don't take the job if she isn't. *He assured me everything was OK. Great. I was giddy with joy!*

On a Sunday morning we flew out to California for a week of training. At the airport he asks me where he could pick up some Dramamine. (This is not a good thing to ask when you're about to pile up about 500,000 frequent flyer miles in the next year.) I just told him to suck it up. (I deserve low points for sensitivity, but high marks for telling it like it is.)

We got to San Francisco, rented a car, and drove to the hotel. We were booked into a Marriott so it wasn't like we were staying in a place with pizza stains on the drapes. I told him I'd meet him for breakfast next morning about 8 a.m. Everything was cool. I got up in the morning and called his room: no answer. No problem, I thought, he is probably out running. I went to breakfast and called him after. No answer. I broke out into a sweat. I went to the front desk and asked if there was a message for me. And, yes, there was, a "Dear Tom letter" saying that he couldn't do the job. It would require too much time away from home, too much air travel, too much this, and too much that. Blah, blah, blah!

It was too early to hit the bar so I went to the office. I walked in and everyone asked, "Hey, where's the new guy?" What could I say? I told them he had quit! The roof nearly collapsed with the volume of laughter! What an experience. My boss was in Europe at the time but he was pretty cool about the whole thing. Whether he was fibbing or not I don't know, but he claimed that the same thing happened to him with his first hire.

There is a short postscript to the story. Later the same day I called the guy to find out what exactly was going through his pea-sized brain. He was practically crying on the phone. Both his wife and his mother-in-law were in the same room when I called. It sounded as if the guy had taken significant amounts of verbal punishment from both of them.

If you think about it, there is a fairly painless way to find salespeople. You have a plethora of people in your world who know salespeople, so why not use them to help you find a person. The following groups *all* know salespeople. Talk to them.

- Other business owners.

- Your customers. *(Asking customers is one of my favorite ways to find sales reps because customers know the difference between good and bad reps.)*

- Friends.

- Salespeople who call on you.

- Mentors.

- Members of your church, sporting group, or any other organizations to which you belong.

- Neighbors.

- Sales trainers in the area. *(Tapping them is my second favorite way to find salespeople.)*

- Selling associations. (In Minneapolis, there is a group called Professional Selling Association. Also, there is also another group called Sales and Marketing Executives.)

- Networking groups. (Many suburban Chambers of Commerce have networking groups

consisting of people with different occupa-
tions. Most of them know salespeople.)

You can place an ad for a salesperson but I would do this only
as a last resort. You will be inundated with resumes and you'll
spend enormous amounts of time returning phone calls and
setting up interviews.

Before you do any of this, however, there is an absolute must.
Think about your company and think about the type of person who will fit into the culture smoothly. *Do not underesti-
mate this or blow off the suggestion!* Consider this anecdote.

*I was consulting for the James J. Hill Business Reference Library
in St. Paul, MN. My task was to hire several salespeople for two
different positions, one a high-level sales position, the other a position requiring all day, every day telephoning to warm leads. The
key was to find salespeople who fit the culture of the library, where
librarians were the core element. No flashy, loud back-slapping,
joke-telling morons need apply. The environment required professionals who were good at reading people, doing the correct sales behaviors every day, who didn't mind working in small offices, and
who did not require a strong emotional support group. We found
our people using six of the above contact groups.*

*My rule of thumb is this: when you find good candidates, the more
people who interview prospective salespeople the better. After all the
reps won't just be working with you.*

Chapter Four

Addressing the Gender and Age Questions When Hiring

"Society as a whole benefits immeasurably from a climate in which all persons, regardless of race or gender, may have the opportunity to earn respect, responsibility, advancement and remuneration based on ability."

—Sandra Day O'Connor

This could be one of those topics that become a legal/HR quagmire! We'll try to stay away from that. I'll start by admitting that I'm sixty-one years young. Enormous amounts of hiring strategies, laws, and philosophies have changed since 1972, when I entered the business environment. The changes have been positive and were needed, but what do you think would happen if today I sent my own résumé in response to an ad looking for a salesperson? No one will admit this, but that résumé would go one of two places, either the round file or buried in a word document so deep in the hard drive your IT person couldn't find it. Sixty-one is still sixty-one even with thirty-plus years of experience.

And I'm pretty sure that if I did get in touch with either the hiring person or HR, they would say that they already identified the candidate and have made an offer. Believe me, that is all they would say. I don't blame them, either.

So let's talk reality here. (You can rest assured that one of the people proofing this document is the best HR consultant in Minnesota.) Age first. An individual who offered me a job in 1983 when I was thirty-eight said that a man's best earning years were between ages thirty-eight and forty-two. Now, maybe he told me that because I was thirty-eight and wanted to hire me, but I don't think so. I've talked with enough friends and business associates about these numbers to believe there is some credibility to them. Those numbers should be expanded to thirty-six to forty-four because four years seems too limited a time period.

We'll return to the thirty-six to forty-four topic in a minute, but let's spend some time talking about age. I have several strong beliefs learned through experience. If you are in the market to hire a salesperson and you can't afford the rep that is used to earning $100K plus, then look for a rep in the twenty-eight to thirty-two/thirty-three-year age group. Chances are this person has had at least two to three jobs out of college, none of which has paid squat, but they have picked up some good experience and are ready to move to a higher level of sales responsibility. This is an awesome group from which to hire a rep.

Here are some other characteristics of people in this age group:

- They may be married and will have either one child or one on the way. *(Or they aren't married and never plan to marry, but they still have responsibilities.)*

- They are either in a house or looking to buy one.

- They are tired of making peanuts, $40K or under. (*When this book makes it into enough hands there may be some indignant cries from those who currently earn less than $40K annually. The reality is that less than $40K is peanuts to a salesperson in his or her early thirties. These salespeople know they can earn more and are simply not satisfied making around forty. If people this age are not earning more than that, then they should look at their skills, the company they work for, and the industry to determine if one of these affects their ability to earn more.*)

- Either a parent or some other reasonably intelligent person has told them that they must start investing in college for their kids, and retirement for themselves, because the "boomers" will pretty much wipe out social security.

- Some of their friends are earning double what they are and it chaps their hides that they're not.

- They are beginning to understand that sales is more than just talking and spewing data, that it takes skill to close business deals, and if they don't learn how to be a professional then they may be forever mired in an average income.

- They are prepared to learn and be coached by others. Age has a way of smoothing over the brashness of youth and the size of one's ego.

- They've decided that they enjoy sales and it has finally dawned on them that they can not only have fun doing sales, but they can make a lot of ka-ching.

- They may have decided on a specific industry and they want to dedicate themselves to being a star in that business arena.

Here's my personal testimonial about how both industry and money caught my attention at age thirty-four. From purely a time perspective, I lost three earning years in the Army from 1968 to 1971. After holding a couple of mediocre jobs, I wound up selling cardiovascular instruments. At the time—1978—I was making pretty fair money, a little over $50K annually. I was a little cocky until I ran into a pacemaker sales rep. For some reason he deigned to talk with me (as a rule these characters were arrogant as hell) and mentioned during the conversation that he made $120K annually. Several things happened simultaneously; my $50K seemed penny ante, and I realized my goal was now to make $100K plus. That conversation had an immense impact on me; it altered how I thought about money. It also taught me that larger earnings come to those who commit to an industry.

Making a lot of money takes a mind-set as much as it takes timing and experience. A lot of people never get to a point in their careers where they believe they can earn that much money. It makes no difference what a person's age is—if he or she doesn't think he or she can generate that much money, then generally he or she won't! My advice to business owners is DO NOT HIRE SUCH PEOPLE. If they can't imagine making significant amounts of money, then they WILL BE SATSIFIED MAKING LESS, which means that their work ethic is questionable. They just don't know what to do strategically to make that kind of money or they can't imagine making that kind of money! Do you want that person working for you?

How do you discover this information about an individual? Well, you could just ask! During the interview, ask the sales candidate what his or her income goal is. If the person is making $50K and he or she says that he or she would love to make $65K, then don't bother hiring the person. If he or she can't imagine earning over $100K, then ask if the person is willing to work hard enough and grow skill-wise, to achieve that number.

So, let's return to the twenty-eight to thirty-two year old. If a sales rep is reasonably intelligent, he or she found a product/industry he or she enjoys, and this person has begun to understand that selling is a profession and is flat out *hungry* to make more money, then they will be a good candidate to assess. Whether you hire the person will depend on how he or she does on the assessments and how they interview.

Should you hire a person right out of college? Not unless you want to change sales diapers every other day! There are plenty of jobs that fresh-out-of-college salespeople can get, including telemarketing, order-taking for a big catalogue house, etc. OK, so there's harshness and a bit of edginess on this topic. If I waffled about every opinion I have, then you'd be wondering if the advice is worth taking. Twenty-three-year-old young adults are not mentally or emotionally ready for a selling position that requires planning, confidence, sales skills, organization, etc. Why do owners hire these people? They come cheap! Don't even be tempted. Like everything else in life there are exceptions, but you'll spend too much time looking for one, so don't bother.

Let's return to the thirty-six year old. Every adage or truism has some holes in it, as does the adage that the ages between thirty-six and forty-four are a person's prime earning years. (A gentleman I know and respect had his best earning years between sixty-five and seventy-four.) I'll concede that there probably are holes, but for all intents and purposes, there is a great deal of truth in the saying. So, do you want to hire this age of salesperson? Yes, and here's why:

- They've learned more than their younger counterparts about how to sell, i.e., they understand more about how to be a professional salesperson. *At some point prior to this age, either they have invested in professional sales training or a previous company invested in it for them.*

- They have more personal maturity, which can translate into a spouse and kids and house payments. Obviously, this can also include those who do not have a significant other. *In the majority of situations, age and experience grow into maturity.*

- They understand personal finances and long-range planning. (At least most of them understand.)

- They may have significant experience in a specific industry.

- They have business and personal reputations to uphold.

- Money has become a huge motivator, though not necessarily an end unto itself. But making money over an extended period of time has become important.

- Just a hint of mortality has snuck into their psyches, as in "I'm thirty-something and I've got maybe ten to twenty years to really make some big bucks, so let's get after it."

- They may have an itch to move into a sales management, general managment, marketing managing, or a CEO role so they know that the experience they are getting now is important to their future positions.

Here are a few more thoughts about these folks. A percentage of these salespeople are born risk-takers, so that if your company is about to take off or has a chance of doing that within the foreseeable future, these people might be willing to work for less money. The potential for stock options, very large commission checks, and/or industry recognition are great lures for certain people. As a matter of fact, many of these salespeople are "action junkies" who enjoy risk and frankly need the rush that these sales environments provide.

The Gender Issue
I have my imaginary HR consultant sitting on my shoulder, so I will walk this minefield with utmost care.

There were few if any female salespeople back in my selling pharmaceutical days in 1973. When you did see one, you almost stared; some of them probably felt a little self-conscious because they did draw attention. Unfortunately, female salespeople were rare at the time.

Fortunately, that has changed. It's no surprise that eventually the good-old-boy network and its members had to die off or become once and for all defunct. There are pockets of the critters still defending their worn-out philosophies but most have gone the way of the dinosaur. There have been stories too numerous to mention about the fifty to sixty-five-year-old CEO, VP of Finance or Sales, or some other person absconding with millions, ripping off the stockholders, cooking the books, or harassing employees. These clowns are on the way out and thank God for that. But there are still a large number of men who will not hire a woman and there is a reason why they won't. They are deathly scared of hiring someone better or more capable than they are. They are fearful of being outperformed by a female who is more qualified in finance, sales, engineering, or whatever the specialty happens to be.

I would never put together a sales team without having a mix of both men and women. Women's brains tend to work differently than do men's brains. Women have some very interesting sales qualities that not all men demonstrate.

To name a few:

- They tend to listen better. (Men have what I call the "leaky faucet syndrome," which liberally translated means "see or hear problem, fix it." In sales it means that as soon as the prospect says they have a problem, a male rep will say "I have the solution." A female rep might wonder why the prospect has a problem, so will ask something like, "What causes the problem?" What impact does this have on a sales call? The prospect talks more and a listening salesperson uncovers real needs! What a concept, huh? Maybe the whole scenario is just a modern-day version of what happened in the caveman era. A caveman killed to eat; the current sales caveman also kills to eat and frankly may not think about much of anything else. No doubt I'll catch some heat for this but, hey, life goes on.)

- Women tend to be more patient.

- They tend to be more organized in terms of paperwork, territory management, and servicing the customer.

- They can be more competitive because they think they have something to prove to their male counterparts and to management.

- They can be more tactful, although the gap between men and women may be narrowing on this one. It seems lately that I have seen an increased number of women who have forgotten that honey attracts bees.

- Some women choose not to be married but they still want the same things their male counterparts want. Those who are married may find that additional earnings allow them and their partners to enjoy more of the good things that money brings to people. This is not a trait, but it does impact why women want to be good in sales.

Here is one personal experience:

In circa 1983 I needed to find a salesperson in the Chicago area. The company sold cardiovascular products. At the time most cardiologists were men and most nurses were women. My goal was simple. (This will sound chauvinistic, but these kinds of decisions apply to hiring whether you believe it or not. My brain just works in devious ways.) I hired an intelligent, aggressive, and money-motivated female. Quite by accident or design (pick one), she was also attractive. Outcome? The doctors liked her because she knew the technology and talked to the docs as if she were another physician; the nurses liked her because she was female and she did a great job of identifying with the nursing staff. Hospitals bought a lot of product in the time she worked that territory. I did interview several men but frankly did not like how they handled themselves during the interviews; plus, the reviews I got from former associates weren't good. I plucked this female sales rep from a job she was happy with. It took some work to get her to make the change, but ultimately she had more fun and made more money with the new job she was offered.

When it comes down to hiring, make an effort to look for both qualified men *and women*. Women can bring different qualities to the job and that blend lends itself to a more open and diverse sales culture.

Let me address one more item before we move on to interviewing. What should you do if all you have are men to interview and they are qualified? Hire one. What should you do if you have a man and a woman interviewing and the man is more qualified? Hire the man. By the same token, if the woman is more qualified, hire her. This is not rocket science, folks! Apply liberal amounts of common sense to hiring.

Chapter Five

Interviewing

"You're only as good as the people you're hiring."

—Pete Waterman

As a first-time manager I did all (or most) of the wrong things. Ninety percent of my hiring decisions were based on my gut instincts. Did I like the person? Would we work well together? Would he or she fit with the other salespeople and the company? These are not bad questions to ask but they focus too much on subjective "feelings" and not enough on objective data.

Before we move into some suggestions about interviewing, let's touch on using assessments during the interview process. *Using an assessment tool is a must!* I have used the Profile XT from a company called Profiles International based out of Waco, Texas. Briefly, their process runs like this:

- As the owner/sales manager, you will need to fill out a job description survey. This creates a benchmark for the specific sales position. Basically, you're creating parameters for the position based on twenty characteristics.

- Every candidate takes an assessment called the sales indicator. This is a quick, down-and-dirty look at how the individual stacks up against five key sales indicators.

- If they pass muster with the sales indicator then they move onto the Profile XT, a longer assessment tool covering a broader range of key indicators.

This hardly does Profiles International's process justice, but it gives you an idea of the essentials. The XT will also give you a series of questions to ask based on the candidate's response to the questionnaire. All the assessments can be done on-line and are reasonably inexpensive. The key to this process is using a certified Profiles International distributor. You'll then get help interpreting the assessments.

Earlier, I also mentioned the DISC profile as another assessment tool. Basically, this assessment looks at four key factors—Dominance, Influence, Steadiness, and Conscientiousness. This assessment not only teaches the salesperson about his or her own style, but it also teaches him or her to recognize styles of other people, i.e., prospects. This is a great tool to help salespeople establish a relationship with the prospect; and relationships are the basis for smart selling. (I'm a high-I, which simply means that my selling style depends on *influencing* people to make buying decisions.)

Whatever assessment you use, have someone familiar with them help you to interpret the results.

Let's Put Them On the Spot
There are some elements to an interview that are, in my opinion, non-negotiable. A sales candidate should be at ease and relaxed, partly because there is no need for the interviewer to be hard-core. Secondly, people will reveal more when they are relaxed. (Bear in mind that there are almost more ques-

tions you can't ask than you can, so listen to what your HR person has to say and stay out of court.)

I usually want to capture a lot of information during the interview. The following is a fairly representative list of topics that are worth investigating:

- What did the candidate like or not like about his or her previous job? *The answers might tell you how the person will react in the job you're offering.*

- What type of customers did the person call on?

- Family. *It is illegal to ask personal questions during an interview. I do not suggest asking about family but typically, in most interviews, the topic of family does come up. Listening to an individual talk about his or her family will offer additional insight.*

- What are the rep's hobbies?

- How did this person sell in the previous job? *Was it a collaborative sell? Was it order-taking with little selling? Did the rep consistently call on low to middle managers whereas your sales position requires calling on higher levels in the organization? It can be extremely difficult for a sales rep to call on the CEO of a company when the rep has been used to meeting with middle managers.*

- What was the sales cycle for their previous product? *Was the sales cycle short while the selling cycle for your product is long? There are differ-*

ent strategies involved with short and long selling cycles.

- Why are they looking for a new job? *Is the rep looking for more money? Was he or she let go from the previous position and if so why? Did he or she have a disagreement with management? Were there few avenues for promotion? Some reps jump around constantly from job to job; they may not know what they want from their careers. A sales pro will tell you what he or she wants.*

- What are these people's earning goals?

- What are his or her personal and business goals?

- Why does the person like selling? If they say because "I like people," shuffle your papers and end the interview. OK, I'm being sarcastic but really there is only one reason people should be in sales and that's to make money, lots of it! Lest the reader thinks that I am purely materialistic let me add that there are many, many salespeople who enjoy sales for another reason: they enjoy selling a product that brings value to customers. I will not argue with that but still, a mortgage, the kids' educations, and retirement beckon. You can't pay bills with good vibes!

The following are other questions I like to ask because they move the conversation away from the feel-good exchange and into the reality of managing a sales territory.

- How do you currently prospect for new business? *Listen for specific answers like "I dedicate three hours per day to phone and network prospecting. I ask all my customers for referrals." If the salesperson balks a little when he or she answers this question, don't bail them out by supplying options for him or her to agree or disagree with. If a rep falters during his or her answer, it would make me wonder if this person does any prospecting.*

- What do you typically say to a prospect on the phone to get him or her to see you? *You do not want to hear that the rep tells the prospect how good the product is and how much money the prospect can save by converting. Preferably, the rep will tell you that he or she does some research on the potential prospect and uses that information during the telephone call to set up the appointment.*

- Set up a role-play scenario where you are a prospect, the sales candidate is making a sales call on you, and this is the first face-to-face meeting. How does the rep take control of the sales call? *Again, look for specifics. Listen to see if the rep uses a process or takes sequential steps to move the prospect (you) through the sales call.*

- How does the rep deal with objections? *If the rep states that he or she usually tells the prospect that a feature of the product will address the objection, shuffle your papers and end the interview! Objections are overcome by asking the prospect a question about the issue and then listening for more information that will shed light on the objection.*

- How do you react when you are losing a good customer? *Listen for specifics like. "I discussed the issue with several different people in the customer's company;" "I determined whether the product was being used correctly;" "I determined whether this was a price issue or quality issue." If the rep says something like "I knocked 5 percent off the price," you probably want to bring the interview to a close. Dealing with price and other objections by lowering the price is illogical.*

- Your customer service rep has massively screwed up an order and your largest customer is taking a look at the competition. How do you react? *I would like to see how the rep says he or she will interact with the customer service rep. Will he or she sit down with the CSR and maturely and intelligently figure how to fix the problem, or will the salesperson flex his or her muscles and berate the CSR for being stupid? The only muscle to use when dealing with an issue between a sales rep and a CSR is the one between the ears.*

- What is your reaction when you hear your territory is being split? *You'd like to hear a salesperson say that there is enormous potential in a small territory, that a smaller geographical area will allow him or her to more effectively tap into the potential. If I were asked this, the second statement out of my mouth would be about how to make the transition to the new rep easy so the customer stays happy. Granted, this sounds like something a goody-two-shoe would say to suck up to the boss, but companies do lose business when one rep takes over part of an existing sales territory. Knowing how to make the transition from one rep to another is important in order to maintain business with customers. If a salesperson has his or her act together, he or she should also ask why the territory is being split.*

- Typically, what do you do prior to making a face-to-face sales call on a new prospect? *In a perfect world, I'd want to hear the rep describe how he or she will do research on the company prior to making the call, research that will allow him or her to understand the company, the marketplace, and the specific contact the rep will meet. Most sales reps do not understand that preparation is 75 percent of the sales call. The better you prepare, the better questions you ask. The better questions you ask, the better the sales call.*

This is a bit redundant, but it is worth stating again. The absolute best way to determine what a rep is made of is to test him or her in a selling situation. As a sales rep this is not necessarily fun, but as a manger it is essential. Give your candidate a pen, pencil, notebook, a magic marker—anything—and ask them to sell that product to you. Listen to how they execute the sales call. Do they ask intelligent questions? Do they listen effectively? Do they identify problems you're having with the product you're using now? How do they close the sale? Do they ask for the order? If a candidate starts to spew features and benefits, a little warning bell should toll in the back of your brain. Selling is not about listing features and benefits; selling is about asking questions, creating dialogue, and listening.

Getting Other Sales Reps Involved

If you have other salespeople in the company, have the potential rep ride with one of them. Your existing rep will:

- See how the new person reacts during sales calls.

- Get a feel for whether the new person will fit into the company culture.

- Have a chance to ask some of the same questions you asked.

- Listen to the types of questions being asked by the sales candidate.

- Get below the surface to see what this person is really all about.

Your sales rep should also take the prospective salesperson out for dinner as part of the ride-along. People tend to relax over dinner and a glass of wine. You will find out quickly if the persona the potential rep presented during the day is the same one he or she presents over dinner. In other words, does the professionalism carry over to social settings?

I was consulting with a company several years ago and I set up a "ride-along" for a rep we considered hiring. The company rep was a devout Christian gentleman. His worst swear word was dangit. During the two days they worked together, the sales rep interviewing for the job used the F word continuously. Needless to say he didn't make the final cut. He failed the culture-fit part of the interview.

Set Expectations

The following suggestion is important. When you're interviewing, don't paint a rosy, blue-sky snapshot of your company's reality. If that version doesn't come true then the new rep will be all over your case, and should be, for that matter. The chances will be good that the rep will move on. Tell a prospective salesperson the truth about the job, the marketplace, the customers, the competition, etc.

Here are some typical blue-sky comments you'll hear from owners or sales managers:

- On average the reps here make six-figure incomes.

- Almost every company in the area can use our products.

- We have about 40 percent of the market, so our name is familiar to everyone. You won't have a hard time getting in to see people.

- The territory you'll have is the fastest growing territory in the company.

- We have a liberal entertainment policy.

- We've had no turnover of the sales staff.

All right, I'm not going to bore you with this stuff. Just be aware that salespeople are smart and they have heard some whoppers when interviewing. It is difficult to fool good salespeople because most of them will ask you questions that are important to the professional. Here's a sampling:

- How is the commission calculated and when is it paid?

- What major snarls or problems have key accounts experienced with your company?

- How do our products compare to those of the competitors?

- Is this a price-sensitive marketplace?

- Will the base salary stay the same or will it be lowered when I begin to generate sales?

- Does the company do active marketing, and if so, how?

- What customer-relation software does the company use?

- Is the company profitable?

- What has been the turnover rate among the salespeople for the last three years?

- Does the company develop new products on a regular basis either through R&D or acquisition?

- What is the reimbursement policy for expenses?

- Does the company encourage entertainment?

- What does this territory generate in volume now? What has been the growth rate for this territory?

- How much travel is expected? Where do the salespeople stay when they travel? *(If you are used to Marriott's, the Motel Six doesn't cut it!)*

During a recent consulting gig I had to hire an inside sales rep. Throughout the interview process I consistently painted a realistic picture of the job. I told the candidate that he would work alone in an office, he would be on the phone six out of the eight-hour work day, the air conditioning wouldn't cool a closet, the offices were overheated in the winter, and parking would cost him $10 per day. We went through this drill several times until I was sure he understood reality. I never received a call from this gentleman about why the actual job differed from my description! It didn't. He knew just what he was getting into.

There is another situation worth mentioning that owners and sales managers forget. What if you honestly don't know the answers to some of these questions? This does happen. For example, there is nothing wrong with saying that you don't know how much travel is required or that price sensitivity is not an issue yet. Perhaps the company is too new and these situations and/or others have not been a factor. You might as well tell it like it is. After you hire someone you do not want to hear, "You never told me about this…"

There is another reason why it pays to be driven by details during the interview process. As an owner and manager you have someone's future in your hands. Now, that may sound sappy, but it is the truth. You should turn a person down for a job if he or she doesn't fit or aren't capable of handling the sales job. It is best for you and for the salesperson. He or she won't waste time and get a bruised ego by being in the wrong job.

I have been in positions when I have not hired an individual I have interviewed several times. I usually try to help this person out by giving them the names of other people who may know of other job openings. There is an outstanding adage that applies to this situation as well as to most of life:

The More You Give The More You Get.

Chapter Six

So You've Got the Right Salesperson or Salespeople— Now What?

"The future depends on what we do in the present."

—Mahatma Gandhi

You will be tempted to not take the following advice to heart but don't fight me on it, OK? And I bet you're thinking to yourself, what's got under this guy's skin? What chaps my hide is the number of salespeople who are hired and told where the executive head is, but then are left alone to figure out everything else. What's the burr under my saddle? Companies don't prepare their salespeople to be successful.

Top professional athletes and coaches prepare for games by studying their opponents. Builders don't erect homes unless they have plans. Banks don't lend money to businesses without conducting due diligence. Investors don't write checks without seeing a business plan and financials. Salespeople deserve and need the same kind of preparation.

So why on earth would a company, after hiring a salesperson, give him or her a catalogue, some account records, a phone book, a cubbyhole of an office, and then tell him or her to get after it? Well, the answer is simple. Owners of such companies and many sales managers as well have no clue about how to *prepare* a salesperson to be successful.

I'm pretty sure I know what you're thinking. If you hire a sales professional, then that person will already know what to do, so why should the owner have to take responsibility for that? It seems logical but it isn't. Here are several more examples of what I'm talking about.

One of the great jokes, in my opinion, in the investing and real estate business is the huge turnover in sales personnel that these industries experience. I've heard that the fallout in either of them pushes the 60-70 percent level or higher within the first six months. To me this has always seemed ludicrous. Why bother to hire people you know will fail two-thirds of the time? Isn't it the responsibility of the company to help people be successful? I know what the response will be. They'll say that most of the people they hire are not the right candidates for those particular jobs, even though they've passed all the necessary licensing tests. Well then, why not use assessments to identify the right ones and then prepare them more effectively for the job? Add the cost of selling to all this and it makes you wonder, doesn't it?

The better you prepare a new salesperson for success, the more likely they will be to succeed. Here are a few suggestions:

- Document a training program around the product, its features and benefits, the market-place, the reasons why people buy the product, and the people who usually do the buying.

- Take the time to familiarize the salesperson with a CRM-customer relation management system, assuming you have one. (e.g., ACT, Goldmine, etc.)

- Point out to the rep using the CRM or other system who the salesperson's key accounts are and why they are critical customers.

- Build a plan to call on the accounts to minimize the loss of business between the rep that was calling on these accounts and the new rep. If this is a situation where an existing territory is being split, have the existing rep introduce the new rep to the key accounts. A smooth transition is critical if you want to maintain the business. If there was not a rep previous to the one you are hiring, still familiarize him or her with key accounts, if they exist.

- If you have customer service reps, have the new sales rep sit in on phone calls the CSR deals with. It's a great learning experience.

- If there is a defined territory, make sure the new rep knows the boundaries so the new person and reps from adjoining territories aren't calling on the same people accidentally.

- Even if there is no territory per se you can prepare a sales rep by helping him or her build a plan to help them manage the territory.

Here is another way to think about this. When you started the company, what knowledge did you need to ensure success in the early stages? Document that and repeat it for each new salesperson.

Success Depends As Much On Preparation As On Execution

This goes for selling as well as preparing a new rep to do his or her job.

Some Horror Stories

The owner in a company I consulted with hired an individual with no sales experience in the industry and zilch sales experience, period. The salesperson spent a few weeks in the warehouse learning what the company sold and had some minor training on the products and how to sell them, then was turned loose on some poor unsuspecting prospects. What a catastrophe! The individual, who happened to be an extremely nice person, was not given the chance to succeed. He had no idea how to manage a territory, to do more than present information, or to use a computer, much less find a customer's record in it. Yet he was expected to produce sales numbers. Lions 1-Christians 0!

Here's a little side effect of what happened in this scenario. The existing sales manager and owner spent enormous amounts of time training, coaching, and traveling with the rep as well as generally pulling their hair out, because the rep did not execute the fundamentals of the sales job. Guess who suffers? Obviously, the customers but also the other salespeople in the company who don't receive the attention they need.

I love this story. Company B was selling a product into some pretty high-level environments. I was brought in to evaluate the primarily phone-based salespeople. As I listened to the salespeople, I cringed inside because they were using the word "guys" when they talked to their P-H-D customers! They'd say "What do you guys typically use when you…." Ahhhhhhh! I practically had a stroke in the cube.

Imagine spending years and thousands of dollars attaining a lofty academic level and some nimrod refers to you and your colleagues as "guys."

When trying to determine how much training a new salesperson needs, let common sense prevail. If your company has one or two products and the person you've hired has significant experience selling a similar product, then you can do without long, involved training. However, if the new rep does not have that experience, then build training around what he or she would need.

In addition to addressing the previously listed areas, I would work with the rep in three other areas.

- Develop a method to work the geographical territory. *If the territory is four city blocks then there is no problem. However, if the territory is half a state and there are 120 active customers, then the salesperson needs a system for covering that large an area. How much time should the rep spend with current customers versus prospecting for new ones? Are there some accounts that don't require consistent visits? Is there a way to work the geography that saves time and expense?*

- Have the salespeople learn a sales process. *Don't just send a sales rep into the jaws of prospects without giving them some professional sales training. The money you invest in this will be paid back within three months or less.*

- Have the salespeople document their goals. *We will get to this subject shortly.*

- Do more than just introduce a new salesperson to other people in the company. Share with new reps how these people impact the salesperson's job.

There is almost a one-to-one relationship between how fast a new salesperson delivers new sales and how much they were prepared prior to making their first sales calls. The better the prep, the faster you'll see new sales.

Chapter Seven

Should You Assume That This Salesperson Has a Sales Process?

"To conquer the art of selling, you need to learn a system."
—David Sandler

Early on in this book I proclaimed that sales is a profession. I'm pretty sure a lot of you still think that I am just blowin' smoke. Oh, but I'm not! I made some analogies with certain groups that are considered professional—surgeons, lawyers, engineers, etc. Obviously, all these folks have gone through extensive training and spent mountains of dollars to become certified to crack chests, to put the bad guys in jail, or to play with the adult version of Tinkertoys.

And yet, what do owners assume after they've hired the sales stud or studette? You got it: they assume that the salesperson knows how to sell. But *this is not always true.* Just because someone interviews for a sales job doesn't mean he or she truly understands the intricacies of selling. Yes, the sales pros do, but again, that's 10 percent of the whole. You may not always get one of these.

There is an old adage that applies to this topic: **Nothing happens until something is sold.** Someone had to buy scalpels, law books, and Tinkertoys for there to be doctors, lawyers, and engineers. There is a not so very fine distinction between prospects buying products based on their needs and a salesperson selling a product that the prospect may or may not need. Most people buy a product because they want or need it, not because some slick-talking sales guy jams features and benefits down the buyer's throat. (OK, that does happen, but not as often now as it did ten or twenty years ago. Buyers are a lot smarter than they used to be.)

Horror Story from Schaber's Past to Illustrate the Point:

Back when Vietnam was still in the news I accepted a job with a certain pharmaceutical company. Several new salespeople went to the home office for product and sales training. During the process, the company taught us how they wanted us to sell, namely by memorizing and reciting a script. Literally, when we were in front of a doctor we were to recite the script while holding a card with the same words on it. How absolutely insane was that? We had to sit in waiting rooms for ninety minutes with a bunch of people hacking their lungs up in order to see some poor beleaguered doctor who would listen to us recite forty-five seconds of practically worthless drivel! Regardless of how inane the sales process was, the company at least dedicated money and time to training. (I still shudder to think that I sold that way!)

That style of selling, my friend, is anachronistic! Flash ahead thirty years and let's check the current batch of salespeople and how many of them sell. Guess what they have now instead of placards? A computer with PowerPoint. It looks cool and certainly is technologically light years ahead of a printed card, but the net effect is identical! Merely spewing features and benefits now is no better than it was thirty years ago, albeit the equipment surrounding the "pitch" is better.

A client of mine from several years ago who we'll call Phil met with prospects from a South Dakota Indian reservation. These folks were raking in some large amounts of money from their casinos. Old Phil was up against some pretty stern competition. I'm not comfortable sharing the names but they were significant players in the investment world. The big suits brought in the power people and the PowerPoint. Can't you see it? Graphs, colors, charts, and revenue promises that would make a saint blush! Old Phil walked into the meetings with a business card, a legal pad, and a pen. He began asking these folks what they wanted from their investments. When he knew what they wanted, he then presented the products that fit their needs. I'm not positive, but he may not have had a computer with him. End result? The little dog chewed up the big dogs and won the business!

The old adage that I like so much should read *nothing happens until someone buys something*. People buy things when they have needs. Good salespeople create a "dialogue" with the prospect, and through tactful questioning and listening, *both parties* agree on what the prospect should do next: either buy or not buy.

Here is an obvious truth: salespeople don't go to school to learn how to sell. They pick the skills up along the way from books, seminars, friends, Webinars, or selling classes. And although all of these methods are OK, none of them instills a system or a process that is ingrained into the salesperson's head. The only university I know of that offers a program dedicated to teaching salespeople how to sell is the College of St. Catherine's in St. Paul, MN. It has a two-year program that touches on all the sales basics.

Before I give you the all-too-simple remedy for this, let me ask you a question. Would you ever consider buying a new computer without the software to make it run? Would you ever buy a two-thousand-dollar set of golf clubs and, without ever playing golf or taking a lesson, walk on a golf course? (I suppose there are a few people who would, but most sane people would not.) Yet, when an owner or sales manager hires a new rep, he or she often never determines if this person knows the fundamentals of selling. You, as an owner, should not take on the responsibility of teaching people how to sell; it's not your area of expertise. You might consider *investing* money to have someone else teach the person how to sell effectively.

During almost twenty-five years in the medical device industry, I worked for six companies. Two of those six put the salespeople through a selling course. It was called PSS-Professional Selling Skills, made famous by none other than the Xerox Corporation. One company out of the six went beyond that and invested in other programs that taught the salespeople about selling styles and how understanding a prospect's social style influences the sales process.

There are more than a few quality selling systems or processes available. But before you go to the Web and search the 7,890,000 (as of 3/23/07) options that pop up when you type in "how to sell courses," let me mention the following. For seven years Sandler Sales Systems franchised me to teach the system pioneered by David Sandler. They have franchises all over the country. *This sales process works!* But if that doesn't work for you, then there is Dale Carnegie, Spin Selling, Solution Selling, Wilson Learning, Miller-Heimann, and a host of others. They are all good and by working with them your salespeople will have a sales process when they finish any of these courses.

My suggestion is to pick one of the above, or another that you feel may fit your industry, and commit your organization to using that system. There are good reasons why you should do this:

- Too many salespeople rattle on about features and benefits without listening to what the prospect or customer needs. *The reason they do that is because most salespeople don't know how to set the sales call up so the prospect talks first about their needs. A sales process will eliminate a salesperson's urge to spew forth features at the start of the sales call.*

- If you manage a salesperson or if you have a sales manager, it will be easier to coach them if you use a system, since each of the reps will then use the same techniques. In effect, they will be speaking the same *sales language*. If your salesperson butchers a technique in a sales call, you can fix it by referring to the right way to execute the technique because you both learned it together during training. (Think of the game of golf. Most PGA teaching pros teach the same techniques to their students because the swing is regulated by certain basic moves regardless of who swings the club. A sales process is much the same.)

- A system or sales process does not affect or change a person's style. The happy-go-lucky optimist won't be affected by a too rigid system. A more solemn person won't have to staple a permanent smile on his or her face because that's what the system says to do. *(Yes, the word "system" does sound rigid! Other words come to mind such as "recipe," "structure," "method," "steps" that convey the meaning I intend here.)*

- A good sales process puts the salesperson in control of the sales call and also imposes the following not-to-be-broken law: DURING A SALES CALL A SALESPERSON SHOULD TALK 30 PERCENT OF THE TIME AND LISTEN 70 PERCENT OF THE TIME. (The world of sales would be a better place if everyone did this. By the way, I learned the 70/30 rule from Sandler Systems and teaching it was a routine part of the training.)

- Every other profession has a process, so why shouldn't sales?

- If a sales rep loses a big sale or closes a big sale, the explanation for the loss or the close lies in how the salesperson executed the sales process.

There are probably more, but you get the sense that I'm a fan of processes. Depending on them makes life easier for you, the salesperson, and the prospect or customer.

Chapter Eight

Sales Meetings and What to Do In Them

"Here's my theory about sales meetings and life; the three things you can't fake are erections, competence and creativity. That's why meetings become toxic; they put uncreative people in a situation in which they have to be something they can never be. And the more effort they put into concealing their inabilities, the more toxic the meeting becomes. One of the most common creativity-faking tactics is when someone puts their hands in prayer position and conceals their mouth while they nod at you and say, 'Mmmmmmmmmm. Interesting.' If pressed they'll add, 'I'll have to get back to you on that.' Then they don't say anything else."

—Douglas Coupland

Ah, sales meetings. Salespeople can't stand sitting through them and too many owners and sales managers spend too much time talking about irrelevancies during them! Believe me, no truer words were ever written. Are sales meetings necessary? Yes. Must they be bad ones? Of course not.

Here are several legitimate reasons why owners should have sales meetings:

- As an owner/manager you need to hear sales-people describing their sales opportunities, where these opportunities stand relative to closing, and whether the opportunities are real opportunities. Too often a week or more passes during which neither the owner nor the sales reps have a chance to connect in person, so meetings provide a good forum to catch up.

- You develop a sense for how fast deals are closing. *If you hear about the same sales opportunities meeting after meeting and reps are not closing deals, there could be something wrong. The sales rep doesn't know how to close them, they're calling on the wrong people, the competition has the business, or the opportunity just isn't there. In a situation like this you need to put the salesperson on the spot and dig for the reasons why the sale is not closed.*

- You have a feel for how well the sales reps know their products and applications. *If you have several products and a salesperson focuses on only one or two that could solve a prospect's problem but doesn't mention other product options, the rep may not fully understand the product line(s). It might be time for a little retraining.*

- You can measure the camaraderie among the salespeople by listening to how they interact during a sales meeting. If they willingly share tips and information among themselves, you can be sure that they are working as a team. *This may sound obvious, but not all sales teams are cohesive. And a cohesive team is an effective team.*

- You can tell by reading body language which reps are losing interest. *If you hear about the same opportunities over and over, that could be a sign that a rep has stopped prospecting. If reps cre-*

ate more and more excuses for not closing business, start to question what they're doing during the day. If one has fewer opportunities than the other reps and if all other things are equal, start to question the person's desire to do the job. If a rep summarizes his or her opportunities with a lot of hesitancy, you can be fairly certain that the rep is making things up as he or she talks. It might be time for a little one-on-one with the salesperson to measure his or her interest level in the job.

- As an owner/manager you can get a feel when the salesperson will need your skill and expertise to help close the deal. Don't forget; the rep may not ask for help but you can tell if he or she needs it by how the reps talk about the opportunity. Also, most salespeople have pride, which means that they want to close the deal solo.

- The salespeople are your best ears for hearing about what is happening in the marketplace. They see competitive products and/or pricing changes first, they hear about prospect's concerns first, they hear about quality issues first, etc. Don't skip sales meetings even if you, the owner, are shackled with many other internal issues. The sales meeting is a good forum to learn about market changes in general.

How Should You Conduct a Sales Meeting?

The best answer is make the meeting short and to the point. Why doesn't this usually happen? The majority of salespeople love to hear the sound of their own voices. (The same malady may also afflict them in front of a prospect.) During a typical meeting salespeople think that every sales opportunity they've had recently is the best one, so they want to talk about it at length. Some of them even love to coach the other salespeople on what they do as if they were the manager. And who knows, maybe they're vying to be the sales manager. This can all involve too much yak-yak. And let's not forget that the owner/sales manager also loves to pontificate about what the reps should have done or not done. Pack all this into one sales meeting and you have chewed up two hours before you can blink an eye.

Next thing you know, the salespeople are grumbling about whether to have sales meetings at all, or they conspire as a group to not mention half the things they have in the pipeline since it will cause the meeting to run long. And if all this wasn't enough, the temperature in every conference room is either hot as the rain forest or as cold as a well digger in the Klondike.

So here are a few ideas about conducting sales meetings:

- Set a time limit for the meeting. Keep it to *one* hour. When the hour is up the meeting is over, period.

- Decide how often you should have a sales meeting. This is not written in stone but I believe that companies should have weekly sales meetings. I wouldn't go beyond two weeks between meetings. *What if you have a remote sales group and they can't be in the office? Ah, technology! Meet by phone; the only aspect you're missing is the body language.*

- Have a set agenda so the salespeople know what's expected of them. *Here is one way to do it. Have the rep summarize the sales opportunity by noting the account name, product(s) involved, potential revenue when closed, date when the sale will close, the name of the person the rep has called on, the next step in the sales process, any objections, the reasons why the opportunity has not closed (if it has been in the pipeline too long), and what the rep might need in the account. (What does "too long" in the pipeline mean? This would depend on the product, the selling cycle, the price, how good the reps are at closing business, the industry, etc. This is a number you will have to come up with.)*

- Cut a salesperson off if he or she starts to wander from this agenda.

- Some mention should be given to competitors and their activities. Save this until the end of the meeting or dedicate five minutes to it at the beginning.

- Don't include training; save that for a different session.

- Listen to constructive feedback about what the company needs to do to provide better support. *This can be a Pandora's Box if not handled correctly. If the salespeople feel that there is a problem with customer service, operations, manufacturing, delivery, the owner, etc., the salespeople need a forum where they explain the issue, the* impact on the customer, *and the effect on revenue for the company. If possible stay away from emotional outbursts and keep the feedback objective.*

Here's how not to handle yourself at a sales meeting:

A long, long time ago when I was a rookie, I was in a sales/marketing meeting with colleagues discussing, among other things, the problems manufacturing had and the disastrous effect the product had on the customer. These were serious issues because a government agency was involved and you just don't want the government poking around your company. We had a series of problems, so you-know-who (me!) shot his mouth off and said something like, "Well, here we go again." As if that wasn't bad enough, I also wrote something similar to management. Well, that little supposed intra-company document wound up as a document that everyone got hold of, to include said agency. It was an innocent and truthful comment but stupid nonetheless. That's enough of the story to serve the point. Keep feedback objective and to the point and leave out editorializing.

- I would have the meetings on Monday morning, not Friday. A good meeting will get people jazzed and ready for the week.

- Vary the location for the meeting. Meetings can become deadly boring if they occur in the same place. Go to a restaurant or have some food catered. Introduce some variety into the meeting. Occasionally, in place of the meeting, have maybe a motivational speaker or a customer come in once every couple of months. Do something to energize people.

- Every so often have other people in the company (from customer service, operations, finance) join the sales meeting. They may or may not have a lot to offer, who knows. The objective is to make other people in the company aware of what goes on behind the closed doors of a sales meeting. It takes the mystery out of what actually goes on behind the doors.

As an owner and/or sales manager you have the responsibility to question what the salespeople say during the sales meeting. By questioning I don't mean interrogating them. In response to what you hear about opportunities, you should feel comfortable posing any of the following questions to the salespeople:

- Who besides your account contact needs to be involved in the decision process? *This is a good question to ask when an opportunity seems to be hanging around too long and not closing. Is the salesperson missing someone in the prospect company's chain of command?*

- This opportunity has been in the pipeline for two months; why isn't it closed? *You don't have to pose the question in quite that direct a manner, but you could say something like, "Are there some other factors affecting the decision to buy?"*

- What problem does the prospect have that our product addresses? Or, what will happen to the prospect's company if they don't buy our product? *People buy for emotional reasons but they rationalize the decision intellectually. If the prospect does not have a pressing need for the product then this is not an opportunity. Don't have the salesperson waste time on these.*

- What's the competition doing in this account? *Have they lowered prices, added value, bundled products?*

- What's the buyer's style? *If your sales rep is a no-nonsense driver that wants the sale now and the prospect is an amiable laidback person who would rather take the process more slowly, there will be a problem. More reason for training.*

- What is the decision process for this company?

- Is the prospect's decision based on price or are other factors involved?

- What will it take to close this business in the next two weeks?

- Why are we pursuing business in this account? *This question should be asked if a salesperson is chasing after small prospects or the wrong prospects. Most companies have a target market, so why waste time on small or non-target companies?*

- Are you seeing the right people? *(A variation on question # 1.)*

- Does this prospect have the budget for this buy? What is the budget?

- Why does the prospect need our product? *(Similar to # 3)*

There are a finite amount of things that stop a sale from happening. Of course, as soon as I say the word "finite" everyone reading this will work hard to come up with an exception. OK, there probably are exceptions, but the following are fairly representative reasons why someone isn't buying:

- The prospect flat out does not need the product.

- The salesperson couldn't sell a life preserver to a drowning man. *There are some obvious hints if this is going on. The salesperson completely misses one or all of the three buying qualifiers: need, budget, and decision maker. The salesperson constantly refers to how he or she has told the prospect that the prospect needs the product. The salesperson says that they just don't get along with the prospect. The salesperson has no clue about what will happen next in the sales process.*

- The salesperson is seeing the wrong person or people. *There is an old adage in sales that says you should start the sales process from the top (with the CEO, President, for example) down and not from the bottom up. It is reasonable to ask any salesperson who the decision maker is? The person running the company has the power to say yes. The people under the top dog can only say no, maybe, or we'll think about it. Of course, if you were selling a new cleaning solvent to Ford Motors, you would probably never make it to the CEO. The decision to change solvents would be made at a lower level. However, if you were selling a new robotic system, then you might want to start as high as you could within Ford Motors. The lesson is to* know *who the decision maker(s) is, what the decision process is, and who will influence the decision maker.*

- There's no money but the prospect doesn't say that, nor does the salesperson ask about budget.

- The product your rep is selling is no better than the competitor's and the rep has not sold the value concept.

- The prospect is using your sales rep as leverage with his current supplier to get a better price, service, or something else.

- The prospect just doesn't like your rep. *Perhaps the rep failed to identify the prospect's social style and didn't adjust his or her style to the style of the prospect. This is more common than you may think.*

- The rep has not identified the real need.

- The rep fails to ask for the business out of either fear or lack of skill.

The owner and/or sales manager has to identify the reasons why a deal isn't closed or what's taking the deal too long to close. If the reason is a skill issue then it is your job to help the salesperson learn how to use the right techniques during the sales process. If the reason the opportunity does not close has nothing to do with the skill of the salesperson, then you will have to look at other reasons, including price, delivery, quality, strength of commitment to the competitor, etc.

Don't think that the owner/manager has to take on the role of "closing cop" and question everything the salesperson says or doesn't say about an opportunity. If the salespeople know the agenda for the sales meeting, if they realize that you as the owner want the same thing as the salespeople, and if everyone is on the same "selling process page," then your sales meetings will be productive.

Chapter Nine

Creating Goals "With" the Salesperson

"The secret to productive goal setting is in establishing clearly defined goals, writing them down and then focusing on them several times a day with words, pictures and emotions as if we've already achieved them."

—Denis Waitley

If you Googled "goal setting" you would find 23,000,000 references. If you want to peruse all these, good luck, and I'll check in on you during the next millennium. Which method is the best? Which one is most thorough? Which one fits your company and sales team? Who knows? Goals are in one sense a moving target. They change, as do the methods to obtain them.

In a minute I'll lay out my version. It is short, not complicated, and can be used for any product or company or person. And yes, achieving my version of a goal will take some time.

Why do the majority of salespeople sincerely dislike goals? Here's a quick list of potential reasons:

- Goals make the salesperson accountable and we all know how the majority of people feel about accountability. *Salespeople should be accountable for their goals to someone else besides themselves. They should be accountable to you, the owner, and to one other person, namely his or her spouse, significant other, mentor, etc.*

- Preparing goals takes time and most salespeople can't sit that long.

- They've tried them in the past and the goals did nothing to improve their performance. *This is probably due to the lack of accountability.*

- Salespeople get frustrated when it comes to thinking and writing about anything not directly related to closing business. *Goals are related to closing business, but salespeople don't always think along those lines.*

- No one ever showed them a reasonable approach to preparing goals.

- Salespeople in general do not understand that goals are directly linked to the amount of money they can earn.

- Salespeople take the time and energy to document goals, but then no one bothers to track them.

I will describe how I work through goals with salespeople. Do you have to use this method? Absolutely not! If you have a better or easier approach to the process, then use it, but just be sure you do something. Without goals salespeople do not have a sense of what behaviors they need to execute to close business. If you don't have goals how do you know what activities to engage in on a daily basis? This is an interesting question. And the answer is that you don't know.

STEP 1: *Have the salesperson determine the income he or she wants for the next fiscal year or twelve-month time period.* So many salespeople make the mistake of determining their income based on the corporate goals they have. Here's an example of that. Let's say that our sales guru Bob achieved his company sales target and that his income based on salary and commissions will be $65K. Obviously, it can be more if he generates more sales. Think about this for a second. Achieving the company goal yields X dollars and at the same time the goal indicates that the rep had to work X hard. Here's a peek inside the brain of Bob. *He knows that if he makes X amount of sales calls and maintains X amount of business and grows business X amount, then he should be able to make the sales goal, which will net him X amount of income.* The logic is sound but the income goal low. Why settle for the income generated if company goals are made? THAT IS SELF-LIMITING!

I strongly suggest that salespeople map out goals for the money they want to make, depending on what their *personal goals* and *living costs* are for themselves and their families. Of course this means that the rep has to sit down and actually think about how much money they will need for a retirement fund, college fund if they have children, grocery budget, house payment, car payment, etc. *In my opinion, salespeople should determine how much* they *want to earn. They should then create sales activities/behaviors based on their goals and not just those of the company. Salespeople need to understand the difference between the two monetary goals.* As an owner or sales manager you should love the sales rep who will use his or her own personal goals as the benchmark for his or her sales activities. Ultimately, *you* make more money.

STEP 2: *Determine what your revenue generating events (RGE) are. This is nothing more than a fancy way to say what represents a sale.* Is it one widget; one consulting project; a piece of capital equipment; computers; a membership to an association? Whatever you sell at a *specific price* determines what a sale or RGE consists of. This is probably the most difficult part of the process because most companies have several products all priced differently. If your product catalogue is six inches thick with three thousand products, this step will be a challenge. We'll look at that in a minute.

STEP 3: *Assign a dollar revenue or average dollar revenue for each RGE (sale) and translate this into commission dollars. (If you have the aforementioned 3000 products, then use an average price.)*

A rep is hired and has responsibility to generate new memberships for an organization. Each new membership represents $600 in revenue. Her task of goal-setting is easy because she has one product with one price. The rep gets a 10 percent commission on every membership. Ten percent of $600 dollars is $60, so if she sells ten memberships per month, her commission will be $600 monthly and $7,200 annually. With a salary of $35K this person will earn $42,200 annually. She also knows that if she wants to generate $60K in income annually, she will have to sell over 400 memberships per year, based on the commission. This is $24K in commissions or approximately $60K annually when combined with salary. Four hundred memberships per year equals about thirty-three-plus per month or eight-plus memberships per week. We'll revisit this in a second.

For the other situation where a sales rep has myriad products at different pricing, the task of determining the RGE is more complex. Hang in there for a bit and we'll return to this situation.

STEP 4: *What is the rep's closing ratio?* Closing ratio is defined as the number of sales calls during which a rep receives a "yes," divided by the total number of sales calls that the rep went on or telephone calls the rep made. Obviously, a "yes" is a closed sale.

Looking back at the membership rep makes this clearer. If this salesperson generates forty telephone calls per day and gets two people to become new members, her closing ratio is 5 percent. Two divided by forty is 5 percent. This is a pretty key factor, as you'll see shortly.

STEP 5: *How many closes will a salesperson have to generate in order to achieve his or her income goal for the year?* This is defined as the number of "yeses" a rep receives multiplied by the commission rate-percentage for one sale.

If the membership rep wants to make $64K annually she'll have to sell or close approximately 480 memberships per year. Four hundred eighty memberships multiplied by $600 per membership equals $288K, multiplied by 10 percent commission equals $28,800. Adding the salary of $35K brings the rep to approximately $64K total compensation.

STEP 6: *How many total sales calls or telephone calls must a sales rep make daily, weekly, monthly, and annually in order to close enough business to make the commission dollars to earn his or her target income?* This number becomes rather large if you think about it. Not every in-person sales call or telephone call will generate a close or even a dialogue. Most salespeople will get a greater number of "nos" or voice mails before they hit the "yeses." I know this all seems pretty obvious but it needs to be stated. I make a point of emphasizing this because not everyone connects these dots in the right way. A salesperson must:

- Make X number of face-to-face sales calls (or make X number of telephone calls) each day, month, or year, which,

- Will end in either a yes or a no or another sales call, which,

- If the rep gets enough "yeses" from the total number of sales calls, will generate commissions for the income they want.

This leads to another key percentage in the process. Our membership rep has to close 480-plus memberships in order to achieve her income goal, but how many total phone calls must she make in order to get the 480 closes? This number is harder to determine because of the following factors:

- Are her telephone calls made to warm leads or are these truly cold calls?

- Is the product "me-too" so there is little differentiation between competitors?

- How good is the salesperson at creating dialogue with the prospect, which leads to a decision?

- How good is the salesperson at creating a need in the prospect's mind?

- Will the price point be an objection and how well does the rep overcome objections?

For the most part these selling issues influence the number of closes and how fast the salesperson will close them.

Based on the closing percentage of 5 percent this rep has to make forty telephone calls per day, 200 per week, 800 per month, and 9,600 per year. Nine thousand six hundred phone calls times 5 percent equals 480 memberships. (For her sake, I'm hoping she has a headset.) And, to make this even more fun, we have left something out of this equation. These numbers assume that every time our sales rep picks up the phone, there will be a voice on the other end! These numbers do not account for voice mail, busy signals, or people who just hang up because they don't want to be bothered.

This example is simplified because basically the clearer the example the better. As a good friend of mine always says, "This is not rocket science, man!" It isn't, but the process of goal-setting does require analysis of the factors we just discussed. How can anyone create an income goal for the year without determining the number of initial contacts, the number of sales presentations, and the number of closes required?

This example also assumes that warm leads come to the rep. We haven't even touched on what a rep has to do to get in front of people if this rep is field-based, not phone-based, so let's continue with the activity a rep has to do if there are no warm leads.

STEP 7: *Determine the type of* sales prospecting behaviors *a salesperson must do in order to get in front of X number of people, to close X amount of business, and to achieve X income.* (We're having fun, aren't we?)

I've said it before and I'll say it again: *if your salespeople do not determine what their sales activities (prospecting behaviors) need to be on a daily basis, how the hell do you think they're going to make their sales goals, much less their own personal income goals?* They won't make either if they do not know what they are supposed to do each day! OK, I've beat that dead horse enough; on to the nitty-gritty.

Here are some daily sales activities that a rep could execute in order to get in front of X number of prospects:

- Cold calling.

- Joining a networking group to get leads.

- Networking with other contacts outside of the networking group.

- Sending out introductory letters to prospects.

- Sending out a newsletter.

- Asking existing customers for referrals.

- Asking prospects for referrals.

- Making presentations to business groups.

- Writing articles for publications.

- Doing walk-ins, assuming the rep is not intimidated by the sign that reads "No Soliciting."

- Hiring a person or company to do the cold calling for the rep.

- Creating an electronic marketing campaign.

These suggestions may not apply to the salesperson who has a sales territory with one main group of customers and prospects. Consider medical reps who call on physicians either in the hospital or office. These reps have a specific number of hospitals or doctors in their territory and the reps usually plan to call on their prospects with some regularity, maybe weekly or monthly. The reps know who the current prospects and customers are, so there is less prospecting than for the rep who has a large geographical area to cover with hundreds or thousands of potential customers and prospects.

Back to the above list. Salespeople must make some decisions about *how many* of each of these prospecting behaviors they have to do on a daily basis. There is no magic formula to this. Some of the variables are the following:

- Will the salesperson make the cold calls?

- Is the industry one where the rep can do cold calls?

- Is the product such that networking will generate leads/prospects?

- Is the territory large enough to warrant doing the above? If the rep has ten accounts, then most of these prospecting behaviors are unnecessary.

- Is the rep mainly farming existing accounts? Perhaps a territory has fifty customers of varying size with enough potential for new business; a rep may not have to prospect for new customers in such a case. In a sense, though, the rep is prospecting, but he or she prospects within existing customer accounts. If I were the sales manager, however, I would not allow a rep just to farm; they would have to also hunt for new business outside of the fifty-customer base.

- Does the company actively advertise in publications, so leads come in for the salespeople?

- Is the territory so large that the rep can't do walk-ins?

You get the idea. As a sales owner or manager, you will need to look at:

- The industry.

- The product.

- The skills of the salesperson.

- The size of the territory.

- Marketing initiatives.

- The nature of the sales calls. Capital equipment sales, for example, require contacting a wide range of people in the same company, where the sale of commodity products requires contacting a wider range of companies.

In addition to all of this, your sales reps have existing accounts they have to service, which means that they will have to spend time with them to grow and protect the business. In this type of situation, the goal is to find a happy medium between prospecting and account maintenance.

As much as you want someone to provide the magic numbers to do X number of cold calls and X amount of walk-ins combined with X amount of networking, it's not possible. Every industry and company has different situations that drive prospecting behaviors.

STEP 8: (Quit complaining, this is the last one!) *No goal program is complete without a way to check progress, so I strongly suggest that sales reps maintain a journal in which they track the effectiveness of their prospecting behaviors.* OK, now that you've read that bit of information, here's the reality. I've managed, coached, and trained a large number of salespeople and very, very few of them take the time to document what they do in a journal. It's the nature of people not to want to take the time to do this and no amount of cajoling, beating, or persuading will probably change this. But try!

Is the "journaling" idea still a good one? Without question, it is. So, what are the options? One is to have the owner meet with the salesperson on a regular basis to review the rep's sales activities and whether the sales activities generate the sales appointments. Is the mix of prospecting activities adequate? Is the salesperson doing the right quantity of the specific prospecting activity? Are enough appointments generated? Two, make the journaling exercise easy for the rep to do. Fifteen minutes a week is all it takes to review and document what a salesperson did during the week. How you do that will be up to you and your reps.

OK, so you have probably had just about enough of the goal-setting topic. I have two more things I want to offer. I've used the example of the membership rep selling one product. With one product it is easier to determine sales activities and resulting commissions because there is one price point.

If the rep has thirty products of varying prices, how do you determine price, and how do you determine the number of sales calls the rep would have to make to get the closes, etc.? The only way I know to do this is to average the selling prices for certain groups of products and use that average price to figure out how many closes the rep will need to make his or her income goal. There is no easy way to do this and in fact there will probably be situations where it is almost impossible to do this. My suggestion is to start with a fairly representative sale's dollar number and put the sales activities to work for a while to see if activities and pricing equal desired income. This is generally known as a S.W.A.G.: Scientific Wild Ass Guess. OK, I admit that this is not a great answer, but it's the only reasonable one I have.

My last comment is this. **If a sales rep knows what sales activities he or she has to do and the rep does those activities routinely and follows a systematic sales process, he or she will always make the company goal and the rep's own income goals.**

If I were an owner of a company or a sales manager and if I were reading this for the first time, I might be a bit suspect of the last comment. How can the author know this? I know because I have watched salespeople execute the right sales behaviors in the right quantities using a quality sales process and they *always* made their income goals. The trick, again, is to know *what specific sales activities* the person has to do combined with the *amount of those activities* needed to be performed daily, weekly, and annually.

It sounds so easy, doesn't it? Obviously, it is not. You're not dumb enough to believe it's easy and I'm not dumb enough to tell you that the process is easy. If you find an easy way to make a lot of money, please keep me in the loop.

Prior to this book going to print I reviewed it to see if I wanted to make any changes. There were a few minor ones. However, I wanted to add in this section a suggestion to read a book called *The Secret*. The short synopsis is that the book talks about visualization and the importance of doing that to achieve goals. It's worth the read. I personally have been doing this for years and it works.

Chapter Ten

Creating Sales Territories

"Common sense is an instinct. Enough of it is genius."
—George Bernard Shaw

There are a fair number of fun and challenging exercises that owners/managers do, but creating territories is probably not one of them! There are as many ways to create territories as there are companies. Here are a few ways, followed by some wisdom:

- By zip codes.

- By city.

- By streets or highways.

- By states.

- By regions of the country.

- By product line.

- By industry, or as the marketing gurus call it, silos. (I'll get to this in a second.)

- By first-come-first-serve, otherwise known as chaos.

- By account.

For all my sales and management career I was what was called a "remote rep," which means that the company I worked for was not located where I lived and I was the local rep for the company. I usually had parts of states or several states to cover depending on the size of the company and how many products I sold.

Several years ago I did training for a local radio station and their method struck me—but not them—as chaotic. Every one of the reps had his or her own book of business. If a rep wanted to call on a new account, he or she had to first check to see if that account was in someone else's book. If it was not then that person had six months to develop business in that company; if he or she did not develop business, then the account went back into a general pool and anyone could take a shot at it. Of course, if the account was in the general pool, then a person could take it but, again, they had six months to make something happen.

The system worked for this station, which is the point. W-H-A-T-E-V-E-R W-O-R-K-S is the rule of thumb.

Here are some additional words of wisdom:

- If your company sells primarily in a metro area and you have the proverbial two-inch deep catalogue and can sell to almost anybody, then divide the metro area up by geography: cities, zip codes, or a combination of both separated by streets or major highways.

- If you have one or two capital equipment products and only larger companies use this product, then create territories from several states. How many? That will depend on the amount of time it takes to close the sale, how good the product is, how good the competition is, what the product will do for the institution and how many accounts can actually use the product. (Obviously, this is the type of sale where the salesperson makes face-to-face sales calls.) *Here's a warning! Don't create an area so large that the salesperson is overwhelmed. In the rep's frenzy to get around to all the accounts, the rep won't spend quality time where he or she should. The reverse is also true; if the rep has too small a geography, then he or she will be banging on the same doors incessantly and making customers angry. I hate to keep saying this, but it depends on the situation and the above criteria.*

- If the budget is tight and you can only afford one phone rep, then there is no point in having territories. Depending on corporate goals and other criteria, let the rep call where they want.

- If your product is used by a specific group—airline, automobile, aerospace, medical, computer—then the number of companies within that industry that need to be called on will determine territory size. More than likely the territory will be a region of the country.

- If your sales force is primarily phone-based then the solutions are similar. I would carve the country up by states. *Here's another warning! When you assign states to a rep, try to have the*

*rep understand the nature of the area they're call-
ing into. Why? Because selling is about establishing
relationships and if you cannot establish one with a
prospect, the prospect is not going to buy. Here's a
classic example. A client in Minneapolis hired a rep
to call all areas of the country. The rep talked so fast
most people had a hard time tracking what he said.
He also had a hard edge to him which the customers and prospects didn't care for. Imagine how this
style worked when the young lad called into the deep
South! And he wondered why so many people hung
up on him.*

This list hardly covers all the options, but from it you can get
a sense for how to establish territories.

There will come a time as your company grows when the
current reps are stretched mighty thin; they have a decent
amount of existing business and their territories are growing, but you can see that the reps have a hard time servicing
accounts and developing new business. In this situation you
have to make the decision to split the territories, i.e., hire
another rep to take responsibility for some of the accounts in
the established territories.

Here are some guidelines for when to split an existing territory:

- The sales rep spends so much time servicing
  his or her existing accounts that he or she has
  little time to prospect for new business.

- The rep spends too much time driving or fly-
  ing to all their accounts.

- The territory experiences a decline in business because the competition has made inroads in those accounts when your rep failed to service properly because of territory size.

- Growth has slowed to low single digits in the territory.

- Sales might be up for one product or group of products, but sales are down in the majority of other product lines. The rep is spending too much time in one specific area and again cannot adequately cover other accounts and product lines.

- You notice that the rep looks like he just did a triathlon in wing tips. He's got dark circles under his eyes, sports a pale complexion, falls asleep in sales meetings, and has little or no energy. This is a salesperson who can't handle the size of the territory. Cut it.

How Fast Should You Grow the Sales Organization?

In my opinion there really are no hard and fast rules to guide you. So much depends on the product, its value as perceived by the marketplace, the size of the individual territories, the sales cycle, and the quality of your reps. I would always err on the conservative side and add salespeople slowly unless demand for the product proves extraordinary. I've seen too many managers add too many people too quickly, which puts strain on a company and the owner.

If you were hoping for a magic formula here, I am sorry to disappoint you. Call me and I'll come visit and we'll work through it together.

Here is a quick anecdote on hiring too quickly:

I made the mistake of hiring too quickly when I needed to split a territory in the southeast part of the country. Growth was fantastic in the company and we needed an additional rep. I was having difficulty finding the right person and was getting some heat from my boss to get a rep on location fast. So I hired a guy with tons of experience. Good news, huh? What's that old song, "Bad Moon Rising?" This guy had a chip on his shoulder, a Napoleon complex, the customers didn't like him, and to really make me feel like a winner, the guy was double-dipping, i.e., holding two jobs at the same time. I fired him and of course he sued. Someone wrote a goodbye-don't-sue-us-check and the nimrod went away. Lesson learned: hire when you need to, but take your time hiring regardless of the fire-eating dragon of a boss breathing down your back.

Chapter Eleven

How To Get Rid of a Rep Without Losing Your Shirt

"My main job was developing talent. I was a gardener providing water and nourishment to our top 750 people. Of course, I had to pull out some weeds too."

—Jack Welch

I can't help but include this bizarre story. It was my responsibility to let a salesperson go. I flew into his hometown so I could do the ugly deed face to face. As we drove up to the hotel, the sign on the marquee said "Welcome Tom Schaber." OK, nice touch! But I didn't think much of it. I met the salesperson in his room and before I started the process, he handed me a brand new briefcase. As soon as I saw the briefcase I knew what was up. He knew why I was in town. He also knew that I had never done anything like this; obviously, he hoped to finesse his way out of being canned. About the time all this was connecting in my brain, I looked on the bed and saw a handgun! I thought "Hey, hey are we having fun yet?" Great, I could see the headline in the newspaper "Sales manager killed when trying to fire a sales rep." I seriously thought of moving back into sales. I fired the man and that was about all there was to it except for the guy's numerous letters and phone calls back to the CEO complaining about me.

This situation taught me quite a bit about the process of letting a person go. Sometimes it needs to be done regardless of how difficult it is. It is also easier to do if both the salesperson and the manager agree ahead of time about performance expectations. The clearer the expectations, the less chance someone has to be let go.

As sure as you're sitting there reading this, I guarantee that you will fire a salesperson or, for that matter, someone from your company or team. It's a given!

If you recall, I mentioned earlier that my gut instinct played a very large role when making a choice of whom to hire. *Sales managers or owners end up firing more people when they primarily listen to their guts during the hiring process than they do when they hire based on a more formal method of identifying candidates for a sales job.* It makes no "cents" (the play on words says it all) to spend the time hiring haphazardly when the outcome will cost you time, energy, and money.

Are you guaranteed never to fire someone if you use assessments, background checks, and comprehensive interviewing? No, but you cut the odds way down with the more lengthy process. Choose your poison; it is up to you.

There are better and worse methods for firing a salesperson. By this time you have probably figured out that managing salespeople relies heavily on specific processes, and why not? Sales is a profession after all. You can't run your company without processes. What made you think you can manage salespeople without them? You need to have and follow a process when you let a salesperson go.

The best way to prove to anyone that a person should be let go is to compare that person's performance with the expectations that you have already agreed on with the salesperson.

An owner/manager and salesperson should ask themselves:

- Has the salesperson consistently met their sales plan? *Yes, there are times when not making a sales plan warrants keeping a sales rep. If the company has not made the financial goal due to some extenuating circumstances, no rep should be fired. If personal issues have legitimately interfered with a rep's performance, the rep should keep his or her job. Assuming that no personal, industry, or company issues have materialized, yet the rep consistently fails to make plan, then you have to consider letting this person go.*

- Has the salesperson failed to service a customer or in some way angered a customer? If so, you have to consider the person a sales liability. Yank 'em! *Let common sense play a role here. By itself, failing to adequately service one customer is hardly enough to fire someone, but if there is a trend toward this behavior and the person has other deficiencies, then taking action makes sense.*

- Has the salesperson created turmoil within the company? *Here are some typical examples. The rep consistently badgers or intimidates a customer service representative, he or she constantly criticizes shipping or manufacturing personnel for whatever reason, or he or she consistently makes demands on the organization that create strife. Most companies have a handbook covering performance and behavior. If the salesperson consistently does not comply with the rules documented in the handbook, and he or she acts in a way harmful to the organization, then dismissal is the only option.*

- Has the rep failed to carry out specific goals or activities you both agreed he or she would do? *Some examples are goals related to sales activities, documenting a weekly sales activity report, specifying revenue goals, completing special projects assigned to the individual, taking corrective action for past behavioral issues, etc.*

- If the salesperson has an expense account, does he or she have expenses for items not typically covered and is this a consistent pattern? If so, he or she should be gone on the next train out of town.

- Has the salesperson consistently acted in an unprofessional manner with other members of the company or a customer, over and beyond those mentioned in number three? If so, then he or she needs to be fired.

Have I covered every situation? Absolutely not! This little foray into a salesperson's errant behavior won't make it into the HR hall of fame, but at least you have a sense of those situations that merit firing a salesperson.

If a salesperson has been around for a while, he or she knows there are only a few behaviors or activities that get them into trouble: he or she is not making sales goals and/or not following company/HR standards for behavior inside and outside the company. Also, let's not forget where probation fits into this process. No one gets fired due to one occurrence unless the behavior is practically catastrophic. Putting a person on probation is a way to give a salesperson fair warning that you as the owner or sales manager expect a change in behavior. If no change occurs then the next action is obvious.

There is a professional way to deal with these situations that will give you some peace of mind and keep you out of hot water as well as the courtroom. Simply put, DOCUMENT EVERY CONTACT YOU HAVE WITH A SALESPERSON, WHETHER THAT INVOLVES A DISCUSSION ABOUT BEHVIOR, COMPENSATION, AND/OR SALES ACTIVITIES.

I know, you're thinking that if you have more than one or two salespeople you'll be spending more time documenting than you will running the company or sales division. Not so. The process is really pretty simple.

The times that you want to document contacts are the following. Several of these are obvious, but you would be surprised at the number of owners or sales managers who miss them.

- Document the initial hiring or offer letter, which contains salary and compensation information. There are numerous examples of these letters. If you do not have an HR employee, an HR consultant will have them and can share examples.

- I would break out the comp plan on a separate document attached to the offer letter. *The document should contain annual sales goals; monthly, quarterly, or annual commission schedule; commission percentages; when commissions are paid; and bonus schedule, if applicable.*

- If you and the sales rep discussed other goals not related to commission compensation, document these as well. *An example might be sales activities where you and the rep agree on the number of sales calls the rep should have weekly, the number of new accounts he or she will have to open, or the method of servicing existing accounts.*

- Whenever you work with the sales rep, document how the salesperson executed the sales call. More on this next.

- If the company has an HR document or booklet summarizing expected behavior, the rep needs to initial that he or she has read it. Do most salespeople read it? Of course not, but their signature covers you.

- If the salesperson is on probation, typically the individual should sign a document describing what he or she did or did not do to deserve probation and what he or she will have to do to remove them from probation.

This process may sound onerous, as if every person you hire will have some kind of conduct or sales behavior that will require intervention. Not true! I would say that there is a very small number of the salespeople on the street who are unscrupulous bottom-feeders whose main objective is to make money from lawsuits. The other salespeople will comply with the objectives, documents, and behaviors that are part of any organization. Of course, you also have a few people that are just too stupid to comply because they really don't know any better. When they've had enough sales jobs to figure out they aren't good at sales, or the responsibilities inherent in that position, they'll find their place somewhere else in the corporate food chain.

Let's go back to number four from the list above: documenting the sales call. Here is an example of what and how to document a sale activity. Let's assume that you are an enlightened owner or sales manager and that you have just spent two days traveling with a salesperson making sales calls. When you return to your office, sit down and summarize what you saw the rep do during the calls. Include the following on the summary:

- What you saw the rep do correctly. *For example, consider if the sales rep did a nice job probing for needs, if they did a minimum of talking during the call, or if he or she set expectations for the sales call with the prospect.*

- What behaviors you saw the rep do that *need improvement*. I use the phrase "need improvement" rather than "did wrong." There is a huge difference between those two phrases.

- Give the rep suggestions on how they can correct the actions you observed in number two. When you work again with the rep in the field, observe whether he or she has implemented your suggestions. If he or she has or hasn't, document the behavior.

- *Always, always, always include positive comments about what you saw and stay away from strongly stated negative comments that derail the person's ego*. Here's an example of the latter. "Jim, what you did with that prospect was horrible. If I had known that was the way you handle objections I never would have hired you." Talk about a whack upside the head with a board! You could just as easily have said, "Jim, I saw what you were trying to do with that prospect when you answered his question on pricing. Could you have reacted any differently to his question?" The chances are pretty good that the rep knew his or her response wasn't right, and is looking for a better solution. You need to set the stage to discuss this. This is easier on the ego and better for your relationship with the salesperson.

- When you suggest alternative approaches to use during the sales call, use the sales process or the *"common sales language"* that the company has adopted (Sandler, Carnegie, Wilson, etc.). I'll cover this in more detail in a following chapter.

Why do I make such a big deal about documenting what you see a rep do? There are two reasons. First you can use the document summarizing what you saw as a way to help the rep improve skills, and second you will cover yourself legally if the rep decides he or she doesn't like you, the company, or the fact that he or she was let go because of the failure to change behavior patterns.

Again, don't think that salespeople as a group are a bunch of whining babies who need their egos stroked 24/7. No doubt some are that way, but most are not. The majority of salespeople want to make a lot of money and, when they don't, they know that, in order to do so, they could use solid coaching and mentoring. Most will be thankful that they have an owner/manager who wants to help in that process.

One more reference to documentation and we'll move on to more positive topics. Let's say that you have a rep you really have to let go due to poor performance. After being fired, the greedy, arrogant clown decides to sue. Any lawyer who sees your documentation of what the *rep did right* and *how the rep needed to improve* will, more than likely, suggest to his client not to pursue the case. Why? The suggestions you made were put into a positive light that were meant to help the salesperson, not put him or her down.

A really amazing horror story:

I encountered a very tricky management situation early in my sales management life. A person I hired, after being with the company for about nine months, began to slide. Sales were flat, if not declining; the rep was very uncomfortable in sales situations and failed to execute some very obvious sales techniques. During this period I religiously documented what I saw the rep do, including effective behavior (and sometimes I had to really search for effective behaviors). This went on for too long, due mostly to my desire to help this person get on the right sales track. Ultimately, I had to let this person go because the sales numbers were significantly lower than any other rep's numbers, and the day-to-day sales activities were not performed. Some interesting legal issues followed. I believe that the reason neither the company nor I suffered legally was because: 1. The person's sales performance for this one rep was extremely poor while every other rep's performance was extraordinarily good; 2. The documentation the manager provided to the salesperson after working with him was very supportive and positive. It showed concern and a legitimate desire to help the rep. The moral of the story is to offer written feedback on sales performance in a positive way that helps the rep grow as a salesperson.

Here's another two cents' worth of philosophy about letting people go. My theory was that I trusted salespeople from the get-go. When I hired a rep I was up front and honest, telling him or her what my expectations were. I also asked the person what his or her expectations were of me. A good salesperson-manager relationship is based on trust and mutual agreement. Are there people who will argue this philosophy? Of course there are. Do I care what they think? Not a damn bit!

Chapter Twelve

What Should You Do When Working With a Sales Rep in the Field?

"A desk is a dangerous place from which to view the world."
—John Le Carré

This could be the shortest chapter in the history of business books. The answer is SHUT UP AND OBSERVE. And you're right; I can't let it go at that.

I can't resist sharing some stories, both good and bad.

Keeping the Mouth Shut
I was working with a salesperson who had an incredible sense of humor. We were sitting with a prospect who wanted to know the dimensions of a specific part of our product. In a matter of seconds we both realized that neither of us knew the answer. In the bat of an eye the rep said, "Oh, that's about an eighth of a fractar." I almost fell out of my chair howling. Obviously, there is no such measurement! The prospect never said a thing (probably didn't want to appear stupid) and we walked out of the call with an order. Me? Never said a thing!

Keeping the Rep's Ego Intact
I was a sales cub in 1975. I had just returned from my initial product training with my new company. My sales manager wanted to spend several days with me. Our first sales call for the day was

at a small hospital in south Minneapolis. It so happened that I had spent very little time driving in Minneapolis so I was not familiar with the exact location of the hospital. Even the map confused me; the hospital was in the middle of four one-way streets. Well, I drove around for the better part of forty-five minutes before I actually found the entrance. Of course, by this time I had pretty much sweated through my shirt. We walked into the office in the hospital and met with a physician who wanted to see a product. Of course, I was still so rattled from the one-way-street fiasco that I opened the product demo case upside down and products flew out all over the place! (In those days the briefcase companies hadn't figured out that it made sense to have the briefcase open one way.) The physician must have known that I was a rookie (the dead give-away was the sweat draining off my forehead) because he just let me pick everything up without saying a word.

This manager was just plain cool. He could have pounced on me for a variety of stupid things I did during the day (there were more), but he didn't. We stopped for a drink after work and we talked about the day. As bad as I felt, he found several things he liked in what I did. I truly appreciated his support.

As the owner or manager, you should go on calls with your salespeople. Here is a short list of activities I recommend you address during and after sales calls:

- Don't immediately bail out the salesperson when his or her knowledge of the product borders on the fringe of reality. The rep may realize the error and correct it or the rep may admit to not knowing the answer. Either way, it's a good learning experience. Obviously, if the situation gets completely out of hand you will need to step in.

- Let the sales rep make the sales call. Enter the conversation when asked to or when the prospect asks a question that only you can answer. *I've heard about managers who just have to open their mouths when they're with salespeople. Before you know it, the sales call belongs to the manager not the rep. You're right; it is hard to keep quiet!*

- Try to avoid answering routine questions when the prospect directs them to you. Simply say something like, "I'll let the rep handle that." The prospect will figure out that he or she needs to communicate with the salesperson.

- Just because you are the owner or manager, don't make promises the company can't deliver, even if you really want the business.

- Talk with the salesperson post-call about what he or she did right or how he or she could have improved the sales call. *You can begin these quick ten-minute sessions with a question like, "How do you think that sales call went?" Keep it simple.*

- During the post-call summary, don't focus just on how the rep needs to improve. Pluck some positive things from the call and mention those as well.

- Travel with the rep enough so that he or she has a chance to receive feedback about where he or she needs to improve over a period of time.

- Make sure that the salesperson gives you a goal prior to making the face-to-face sales call.

I made a presentation to a group of sales managers and I began the presentation with the comment that "managing salespeople is a black art." You talk about hitting a raw nerve! There was a fair amount of laughter and about ten hands raised to ask questions, most of which in some way, shape, or form suggested that managing salespeople was more like trying to herd cats than practicing a black art.

Managing salespeople and working with them in the field does not have to be chaotic or confusing. As an owner/sales manager, please keep in mind that your overriding goal *when working with salespeople* is to *observe the salesperson during sales calls and, based on what you see, to improve the skill level of the salesperson.* Let me give you a little philosophy first and then I'll list the obvious things a manager should do before, during, and after the sales call.

If you believe the comment I just made about the goal of an owner/sales manager, then also think about the corollary: *an owner/manager ideally should not have sales responsibility for his or her own accounts.* It's fair to ask why. It is fairly common practice for an owner of a company to have his or her own accounts that he or she continues to call on. If you think about what drives most salespeople (and owners are salespeople), it's not hard to understand why owners want to keep some accounts. They like continued customer contact and they like commission dollars! After all, the owner:

- Worked hard to get the business in the account(s).

- Developed rapport with the customers.

- Is being paid commission for the business he or she developed from the account.

- Has a sales ego (a good thing), which is fed by hunting for new business or growing existing business.

- Has a gene-driven competitive factor that needs to receive recognition for growing sales.

- Wants to keep competitors out of the account.

- Has difficulty handing over an account because he or she doesn't feel completely confident that another salesperson will do as good a job in the account.

Herein lays a very interesting paradox. We'll return to the topic of what an owner/manager should do when in the field with salespeople, but first you might like to know why so many owners fail at sales management once they assume that role. (See the seven reasons just mentioned.) Similar results occur when salespeople are promoted into sales management. Salespeople are promoted to the sales management role because the owner mistakenly thinks that this person has done well in sales and will therefore do well as a manager. The same reason explains why many owners are challenged when they assume the role of sales manager. In both cases the individual is not hardwired to manage others. I'd like to share a real-life experience that I think sheds some light on this topic.

Let's take a trek back in time to the winter of 1969. I was in the Army and, at the time, had Vietnam staring me in the face. I was in a six-month program called OCS-Officer Candidate School, after which I would be the proud owner of a little gold bar making me a Lieutenant in the Army Infantry. (Believe me, this was not a good thing to be at the time.)

OCS was the most degrading, challenging, and rewarding six months I ever spent anywhere. In true Army fashion, they took this six month period to break you down and build you up to what they want you to be as a leader. Early in the six-month cycle each platoon picked a platoon leader, a position that made the person chosen the target of unending grief from the tactical officers and the mother hen to about thirty other people in the platoon. The choice the platoon made came down to me and one other candidate. I was honored that twenty-nine other people chose me. When I thought about it more, I was also a little bewildered. Why me?

I never did figure that out at the time; frankly there was no time to think about it then. Quite a few years later I had an inkling about why these twenty-nine people made the choice they did. First, let's state a caveat or two here. One, I am no shrink, so I am not licensed to draw conclusions about character traits, mine or others. Two, I am not arrogant. I am confident but I am not wrapped up in my own importance. The situation was what it was and a group of people happened to think I fit the role of platoon leader. Of course, they could also have thought I was a complete butt-head and who better deserved the role! (Like that great philosopher Popeye once said, "I yam what I yam.") So this is not about me, it's about specific skill sets that people have and we all have a specific set of them.

Here is what the platoon leader position required:

- *Working harder and smarter* than anyone else in the platoon.

- Taking incredible amounts of crap from tactical officers who considered you to be their whipping boy for anything the platoon did wrong.

- *Listening* to Billy Joe Bob while he tells you his girlfriend Sally somewhere deep in moonshine territory just married his best friend. (True story, true names.)

- Having the knack for *connecting* with different styles of people and building trust with them. (In this hodgepodge group, we had two guys with master degrees, twenty or so people with college degrees, and seven others with no more than third-grade educations.)

- *Thinking fast* on your feet.

- *Getting more out of people* than they thought they had.

- *Telling people the truth* without making a lifetime enemy.

- *Admitting when you're wrong.*

- *Staying focused* on the next task. If you thought too far ahead, you ran the risk of screwing up the objectives in the near term.

If you think I had all these qualities, you're being too kind. I had some and had no idea the others even existed. I was twenty-four years old, had flunked out of two colleges, yet somehow managed to patch a few brain cells together to graduate from college in five years. Although I did not know it at the time, I had some personality traits that twenty-nine other Vietnam-bound grunts felt would help them get through six months of living hell.

So what does the anecdotal nightmare have to do with the title of the chapter? It explains a little about the characteristics owners and managers need, characteristics that if executed correctly will help a manager or owner do the right things when working with salespeople. If the owner/manager does the job correctly he or she:

- Will *not* teach the salesperson to sell the way he or she does. Most people develop their own selling style in time. *Everyone has his or her own selling style and what works for one person does not always work for someone else.*

- Will assess salespeople on their skills using a "common sales language" as the benchmark. *(Sandler, Carnegie, Solution Selling, etc.) Using one of these systems helps both the owner and the salesperson focus on specific techniques to use during sales situations.*

- Will help the salesperson focus on doing the right sales behaviors every day, week, or month.

- Will allow salespeople to make mistakes. *This means stapling your mouth shut during sales calls. For all intents and purposes, a salesperson can't screw up a sales call to the degree that the situation can't be remedied.*

- Will have the salesperson document his or her goals, both personal and business.

- Will coach the salesperson after the sales call, i.e., discuss what occurred during the call. The manager should focus first on what the rep did correctly, and then focus on situations where the rep needs to improve. Keep the word "wrong" out of the discussion if at all possible. Also, ask the salesperson to describe how he or she thought the sales call went. *Here's an example. "Cathy, I really liked how you created rapport with the prospect. It was plain to see that the two of you got along well and that he respected you. What did you do to make that happen?" Or, "I noticed that you steered away from talking about the prospect's budget. Was there a reason for that?" After listening to the rep's explanation, offer some suggestions about how she could have approached the budget discussion and then role-play the approach with the rep.* This is absolutely the best way to coach people. It is respectful of their approach to sales, it gives them options for the future, it gives them a chance to try out other options, and it creates trust between you and the rep.

- Will create a "trust bond" with each rep. *Your job as the owner/manager is to bridge the gap between you and each salesperson. Different things make different people tick; most people are into sports, friends, family, church, reading, or pursuing advanced degrees. You name it and people will enjoy it. Creating a bond with a rep means getting inside his or her head to find out what drives their motor and then listening to the rep talk about those things. You are not some distant person who has no connection with the people you manage. If you don't believe that, look at your company revenue: the size of that revenue depends on how well your salespeople sell.*

• Will master good listening and questioning skills. *If you think about it, managing/coaching salespeople is not that much different from selling. Managers need to "sell" their ideas on selling, goal-setting, etc., to the salespeople. The better the salespeople buy off on you, the more likely they'll buy off on what you want them to do.*

Chapter Thirteen

Compensation

"It's not your salary that makes you rich; it's your spending habits."

—Charles Jaffe

This is not one of my favorite topics. Making money is great fun and having other people make money is fun, but creating comp plans is not fun. Part of the problem is that creating comp plans is not one of my strong suits. The other is that many owners and companies want to cap what salespeople earn, or if not cap earnings at least make it hard for the salespeople to make the kind of money that they want. (By capping I mean creating a comp plan that limits what a salesperson can earn on commissions.) So, creating a comp plan has to meet several criteria: One, it should be easy to put together; two, it should make sense to the owner, i.e., he or she should make a lot of money but not at the expense of the salesperson; and three, the salespeople shall have an opportunity to make significant amounts of money.

Most salespeople want to make the most money they can and they do not care if they have to work their backsides off to get it: show them the money and they will work to earn it. I did say most! There are some salespeople who don't care if they make average money; either they have low ambition or they have a trust fund that hasn't kicked in yet.

Here is a little homespun philosophical aside that I want to get on the table even though it will ruffle some feathers. *Salespeople should have the potential to earn more than the owner or president of the company!* And in a perfect world, the sales rep may also make more than the sales manager if one exists.

It was circa 1985 or '86 and I managed a group of medical reps, one of whom earned $500K one year and about the same the next year. Me? I also did well but not to the tune of half a mil. The president? Don't know his salary but it was not $500K. Did the president have beaucoup stock options? Yes. Did the president care if some of the reps made more than he did? No, because he knew this simple fact: if the reps made a lot of money, he would too, eventually. In fact, the president of this company was the one who told me that a good rep should make more than the president.

As always, there are exceptions to this rule of thumb. Should every rep make more than the president/owner? No. Poor sales performance should yield poor pay, moderate effort should yield average pay, and outstanding effort should generate the best earnings.

Here's the corollary to the first bit of philosophy: Keep the compensation plan simple. *One company I worked for had three levels of commission: a low percent basically for maintaining the business, a higher percentage for any revenue over the previous year's goal, and a higher, third percentage for all revenue over the current year's goal. That third percentage looked very, very good at the beginning of the fiscal year until you broke it down and realized that you'd need spiritual intervention to make it over goal. If you did make it over goal there were only fifteen shipping days left in the fiscal year when the high percentage kicked in. Ah, the sordid, creative mind of the sales manager to create a comp plan only a physics Nobelist could figure out.*

A reasonable comp plan pays the sales rep a fixed percentage from dollar one. Let's assume that the commission percentage rate is 5 percent. For the month of January our rep Billy Joe Bob generated $100K in sales, which means his commission is $5K for the month. In February the process starts all over and the 5 percent is paid from dollar one starting on February first. If the rep generates $75K in sales, the commission would be $3,750. Every month the commission is figured out based on the sales dollars for that month.

The second part to this plan is to have an annual bonus dependent on the sales rep making the company's sales target. If the annual sales target is truly challenging, then the annual bonus should be sizable. So, what's sizable? Good question. $10K? $25K? $75K? If the salesperson has worked hard, brought in new accounts, grown the existing accounts, brought leadership to the table, sold a higher percentage of new product offerings than the other reps, beat his or her corporate goal, and generally performed like a star, then why not pay him or her a large bonus? The more the reps make, the more you make as owner or sales manager.

I will tell you that this plan is very good for the following types of situations:

- When the company sells high margin products.

- When the number of products offered are few and the margin is similar for all products.

- When the company is small and it wants to take market share away from several competitors ahead of it.

- When the company is large and they want to keep competitors out.

- When some or all the products are reasonably high tech.

- When all or the majority of salespeople are professionals and motivated by money.

The next question you're thinking is whether the salespeople in this situation should have a salary? The answer is yes, although it does not have to be a large base. Again, there are variables here. Salaries are good when:

- The company and/or product is new and the revenue is also probably small. The rep has to live on something as he or she generates new sales.

- The rep just hired is new to the industry and it will take time to learn the product(s).

- The product sales cycle is long.

- The company has passed the early start-up stage but can't afford large salaries. The majority of income for salespeople will come from commissions.

- The sales effort required is one of protecting current business or growing business marginally.

- The job is phone-based; requires tele-prospecting; and the salespeople are young, inexperienced, and think that receiving a regular salary is like having weekly keggers. This is a classic situation in which the owner is taking a lot of money out of the business and doesn't care what the salespeople make. Turnover is probably high at this owner's company.

If the commissions the salespeople earn are high, then the salary should be low or non-existent. If a rep is making several hundred thousand dollars a year and he or she has been doing that consistently in a strong company and industry, then forget the salary.

If the company is small and is generating a small amount of revenue but has a huge potential for big sales, then put the rep on a base salary but pay out a large percentage in commission dollars. Once the rep is generating six-figure sales revenue, do you continue offering a salary? Based on what I just wrote, no.

Here is another scenario. I've seen too many situations where a sales rep makes a good salary, say $75K annually and, although he or she generates sales, the rep isn't setting any records. For this scenario let's assume that there are no commissions, just salary. The rep's performance is average. If the individual is OK with that salary, then what will motivate him or her to prospect and close more business? The answer is simple: nothing. This situation is just as bad for the company as it is for the salesperson. The owner has expectations that sales will rise but the rep is happily going on his or her merry way collecting paychecks every two weeks. I know that there are sales positions where companies only pay a salary and if there is an annual bonus it is small. A salary-only job may be one where the sales rep has minimal responsibility for growth but, instead, must maintain significant amounts of business.

I'm sure those jobs are out there; I just wouldn't want to have any part of them.

The Disappearing Salary Trick

Let's take this situation. The company is small: let's say they have sales of two million dollars annually and they have just hired an experienced salesperson. The rep won't start at rabbit wages, so the company offers the salesperson a salary of $80K but after six months the salary will be reduced by $30K. After one year it will be reduced by another $20K. The theory is that by the end of the sixth month the rep will be generating enough new business to make up for the $30K decrease in base salary. In the beginning the burden is on the company but later the burden is on the salesperson to generate sales. For the right salesperson this can be very motivating.

If you think about the information I've offered about professional salespeople versus the rest out there, some things are self-evident:

- If you want to staff your companies with professional sales representatives, then prepare to pay them well. The cream of the crop will not even talk to you if there isn't a six-figure potential on the table.

- You pay for what you get. (Does that even need explanation?)

- Straight commission jobs will result in extremely high turnover. Think about real estate brokers, stockbrokers, and car salesmen. Stay away from offering commission-only jobs unless you really enjoy hiring. *Of course the excep-*

tion is the case where a proven sales pro has worked away from a salary because they are generating large commissions.

- Be consistent with the commission percentage; don't pay one person at a 3 percent rate and another at 6 percent. Salespeople talk and you'll end up having a lot of explaining to do.

- Don't reverse course on the commission plan by starting off with a good plan then changing it when you realize the salespeople are making too much money.

- If you pay well and the word gets out, then you'll never have to spend much time finding salespeople; they'll flock to your doors.

Draws

Many companies do not pay a salary but they do offer a draw, which is similar to a salary. Basically, if the salespeople generate enough business every month and the commissions they earn are greater than the draws (salary); the salespeople keep their draws, like they would a salary. If a rep does not earn enough through commissions to cover the draw then the rep owes the difference to the company. I'm not a big believer in draws, probably because I've never been on one. The other reason is that the draw can create unnecessary pressure for salespeople. They end up thinking more about whether they'll cover the draw then they think about selling. So, let's talk a little about pressure.

Pressure, Sales, and Compensation

Selling is, by its nature, a pressure-filled job. There are no guarantees that customers won't switch to the competition, that a new product won't capture the imagination of the marketplace, that the company won't be sold, or that the company in its infinite wisdom won't shrink territories so income levels plummet. If you can think of it, it can happen.

All professions have pressure attached to them but, in my opinion, selling has the most. I'm probably prejudiced, given the fact that I've been in sales for over thirty years. It's that level of uncertainty that eventually drives a lot of people out of sales. *(As I read through this last statement it does sound a tad on the cavalier side. Surgeons cracking chests, $600-per-hour attorneys preparing for billion-dollar law suits, and a host of other occupations all have incredible amounts of pressure. These cats are still getting their dollars though, at least until the quality of their work decreases. Your friendly salesperson has to make a sale before his or her commissions kick in.)*

I raise the topic because I believe that there is enough pressure in sales without worrying about income. I'm not suggesting that salespeople should be paid so that there is no pressure on them to perform; that's economic suicide. Salespeople choose sales because they want the opportunity to make money and most salespeople know that there is pressure inherent in the opportunity to make money. However, no one wants to work in an environment where hard work yields substandard income or where owners look out more for themselves than they do the people who generate the sales for the company.

If salespeople know that their hard work will generate above-average income they will go to the mat for any owner or manager. Give them that environment and they will make everybody rich.

Per usual I have one final comment. You can find volumes of information on compensation plans that will provide more options than you have the time to read. Keep in mind one thing—keep them simple!

Chapter Fourteen

So Exactly How Do You Manage (Connect With) Salespeople?

"To handle yourself, use your head; to handle others, use your heart."

—Donald Laird

I was managing a group of salespeople and I inherited a sales rep older than I was. Does the phrase "grizzled veteran" ring any bells? Here I was, a cherubic, fairly-wet-behind-the-ears manager and I'm sitting across from a guy who looks like he would enjoy gargling with tacks! He was also a damn good salesperson who had made well, and I mean well, into six figures several years running. Bill (not his real name) was a sales stud.

The sales job called for the salespeople to write a weekly call report describing their activities during the week. As I sat across from Bill for our initial rep/manager meeting I decided that it would be plain stupid for me to ask this guy to do a call report. I already knew that he was a slave to work, putting in ten to twelve hour days. He did the right behaviors, had the majority of the business, customers loved him, and he made himself, me, and the company a ton of money. I looked at him and I said, "Bill, you're the most productive and effective sales rep we have so it seems ludicrous for me to expect a call report from you: so don't bother doing one." You should have seen his face! It lit up! For him, call reports were a complete waste of time and paper. All he wanted to do was sell and make money.

Why would any sane manager force a really productive salesperson to do something stupid?

This gentleman never knew that I had seen some examples of his past call reports. They were scrawled in a shorthand no one knew, covered a smidgeon of what he actually accomplished during the week, and offered no insight into the marketplace or competitive activity. As a manager, why take a stand on something like a call report when a rep is clearly productive and doesn't see the value of one anyway? All you do is really yank someone's chain for no clear benefit either for the rep or to you.

I know, making exceptions is scandalous behavior. We're supposed to treat everyone the same, not do any favors, make no exceptions, and please, while you're at it, don't show your humane side. What a crock! We'll come back to the crock part of this in a second.

I joined a company as a regional manager and the first thing I did was to make the circuit and meet each of the reps. I wanted to get to know them over dinner and listen to what was happening in their territories. Holy shnikies, what a week and a half that was! These people were a-n-g-r-y! Angry at the company, at their previous manager, R&D, production, you name it and these folks were ready to bolt! I made one of those command decisions and just sat, listened, and wrote down everything they said. I had writer's cramp by Dallas!

I knew their previous manager and he was (and still is) a really good guy. At the time he just didn't know squat about what it took to connect with salespeople. This group needed to vent, and frankly most of what they said made perfect sense to me. Yes, some of their feedback was ridiculous and there was a lot of "she said, he said" but the point is, these folks did not need General Patton as their next regional manager. They needed a listener.

OK, before you think I'm a saint I'll mention some bonehead mistakes I made, but first let's go back to the theme here.

The title of this chapter has the word "connect" in it for a reason. Managing and connecting are two very different things. One definition of manage from Webster is "to exercise control over;" another is "to succeed in accomplishing or handling." Nice and warm and fuzzy, aren't they? Connect is defined as "to join." Hmmm! In the context of this chapter the word connect is not adequately defined but even the phrase "to join" is better than "exercising control over."

Your job as a manager is to connect with each of the salespeople so each of them feels that you care about what happens to him or her. *You are connecting with a person not just a job.* I'm not suggesting that you become a wimp walking around with a mushy grin on your face telling your salespeople that you're now their Zen master. Nor am I suggesting that you become the stone-faced, tough-nosed sales manager version of Mike Ditka.

Here are some suggestions to help the connection process:

- Find out more about your salespeople than their social security numbers. What are their hobbies, how big were their families of origin, are they married, how did they meet their spouses? Do they have kids?

- Find out where the individual wants to go in his or her career. Does the person want a company of their own someday? Would the person consider managing? How much money do they want to make?

- Ask the individual how you, as a manager, can best help him or her. *(Of course you may have to pick this person up off the floor when you ask this!)*

- One of the most important things you will ever do as a manager is to take the rep and their significant other out to dinner! (I'll share a story in just a minute.) A salesperson and his or her significant other are in the sales job together. It may sound corny but it's not. They are a team. The spouse isn't making the sales call but he or she is the main support mechanism for the rep. The better the spouse understands you as the sales manager, the more patient he or she will be with travel, meetings, and all the other things that take salespeople away from home.

- Assuming that the rep isn't in AA or some equivalent, have a drink with him or her at the end of a day. Generally speaking, when people have an alcoholic beverage, they loosen up. This is a perfect time to connect with this person beyond just the work environment.

- When the rep closes a large piece of business or does something that deserves mention, give him or her something, a gift certificate for dinner for two, a round of golf at an upper-tier course. I know, I know. Salespeople get commissions, so why do they need any extras? I won't disagree with that, but think how much stronger the connection with the rep will be because you went out of your way to reward him or her with an extra spiff?

- Publicly commend the rep at a sales meeting or in a newsletter about a sales call or some other behavior that the person did particularly well.

I was interviewing a gentleman for a sales job, which meant his relocating and taking a hit on income, at least for the first year. There was risk involved; however, the long-term income potential was enormous. The man was all for it, but his wife wasn't quite as gung ho. Talk about a red flag! So I put my neck squarely in the guillotine and asked them both out for dinner. We did not talk about the weather in South Carolina. I had one job that night and that was to answer every question and address every fear the wife had about the job and the relocation. I didn't soften the impact of changing jobs and relocation by painting a rosy picture full of half truths. I told it like it was and added that I really wanted her and her husband for this position.

The gentleman took the job and did go on to make a lot of money and they both enjoyed their new location. To this day he is one of the top reps and nicest persons I have ever met. I found out later that what swung the wife in favor of taking the job was getting together with the manager and hearing the truth about the risk involved.

Connecting and establishing strong relationships with salespeople is no accident. At the same time I don't believe that every person has the ability to manage salespeople. To be good at sales management one should be or have:

- Empathy.

- Good listening skills.

- The ability to say that you're wrong.

- The willingness to "serve" the salesperson because they are the manager's customers.

- The skill and the desire to coach and build better salespeople.

- Patience.

- Availability when reps need help.

So, here is the caveat to all that. If you're working in a cold-calling sweat shop in New York selling investments, then these attributes may not apply to what you do. However, they should apply to every manager and business owner who cares enough for their customers to hire quality people to sell the company's products.

I mentioned that I also made some bonehead mistakes as I worked to connect with salespeople. I was working with a rep and we had had a long day, so we were enjoying a nice bottle of Pinot Noir. While chit-chatting, I made a comment about another rep in my region. The comment was innocent and not at all derogatory but the rep I was with relayed an altered version of what I said to my other salesperson. And naturally, that person called me on it several months later. As I found out much later, there was a lot more to this whole episode than even I knew at the time.

There is a very fine line between what I call connecting and becoming too close. Sometimes it is tempting to share information, attitudes, regrets, or whatever that really are not the business of the salesperson. Everyone likes to hear a good rumor or a juicy bit of gossip, but trust me, it isn't worth it.

Chapter Fifteen

The Wrap-Up, Some Thanks, and Remaining Bits of Wisdom

"For some, this is the end; for others it is the beginning."

—Unknown

Without a doubt there will be some people who read this and recognize the stories that pertain to them. Maybe that's a stretch, too. Maybe they've forgotten who the hell I am or frankly don't really care. More than likely that's the real truth. If these folks do remember me and still harbor some resentment (assuming the story was not a good one), then here's my advice: get over it. Time marches on. Hopefully by now they've retired or hit the Lotto or inherited Uncle Jimmy's attic full of 1940s and 1950s Topp's baseball cards. If what happened to them during our manager/sales rep relationships scarred them for life, I'm truly sorry. However, the chances are that when the dust settled way back then, these people also received smidgeons of reality about themselves.

Lest I forget, I want to thank some folks who, in their own very real way, provided me with the experiences that helped me write this book. There is something extremely ironic about this as well. There are far fewer quality leaders who taught me valuable lessons then there are complete and total duds, people who taught me how *not* to do things.

First, let me thank a West Coast ex-surfer by the name of Gary Curtis. He promoted me from sales rep to national sales manager. Gary gave me the opportunity to manage salespeople, something I had always wanted to do. Along the way he taught me several things and put me in a position to learn others:

- Communicate effectively with different kinds of people, and how to do it.

- Don't try to salvage every salesperson.

- Reward salespeople by giving them the chance to make a lot of money.

- Keep the comp plan simple.

- Treat salespeople like professionals.

- Taking risks is part of success.

- Listen.

- Families are number one.

And of course there is a story worth telling here. Somewhere back in early 1983, he and I were working in Oklahoma making sales calls. We were driving from Oklahoma City to Tulsa. It happened to be the day when the Vietnam Memorial was being dedicated. As I drove and listened to the ceremony, Gary could see that I was moved by the experience, since I had served there for a year. He offered to drive so I could pay more attention to the broadcast. What made this mean so much to me was that Gary was philosophically on the other end of that war, excuse me, conflict. So here we were, two guys who saw events from different perspectives (at least at that time), and the one who was anti-conflict had the courtesy and sensitivity to be aware of how I was impacted by the event unfolding on the radio. I will never, ever forget that!

The president of the company where both Gary and I worked was a gentleman by the name of Bob Riese. At the time when Bob came on to lead this company, I was experiencing some career doubts. If my memory serves me right I had gone so far as to interview with another company. Robert and I sat down for pasta one night and he, in a very nice way, raked me over the reality coals. The issues were important then but not worth summarizing here. Bob taught me a great deal about family, money, time, risk, people, long-term stock gains, and a whole bunch more. Even though he was not that many years older than I was, I felt like a wayward son who needed some strong, fatherly counseling. Robert passed away not long ago. Many, many people will miss him.

There are many, many salespeople with whom I worked over the years who should receive some ink here but won't because I simply can't name them all. These salespeople and those who supported them were the reason why we all were successful and made more money than we ever dreamed of. I'll let it go at that. Ya'll know who you are!

It's finally time for me to wax eloquent on a few things (as if I haven't already). I'm entrusting something to all business owners and managers who have salespeople. Professional salespeople are unlike any other group of people you will ever know! They come in all different styles and exhibit some or all of the following characteristics: They are

- Maddening.

- Egocentric.

- Slaves to work.

- Motivated by money.

- Motivated by recognition.

- Dedicated to family.

- Dedicated to customers.

- Prospecting gurus.

- Guaranteed to always side with the customer.

- Perfectionists.

- Stubborn as mules.

- Willing to give their collective shirts off their backs to help people.

The list could go on. Suffice it to say that salespeople are the cogs, the engines, the fuel—whatever metaphor makes sense—that drive sales. Treat them with respect, pay them well, and minimize their hassles and they will make you a lot of money. Amen to that!

And, finally, my last comment and disclaimer. I have not stated or implied in any of these pages that this book will be the only book you will need in order to understand all the facets of running a sales organization. If anything, I have stated otherwise in several chapters. The book offers a *practical* guide to help business owners and sales managers move through the sometimes frustrating tasks of finding, hiring, interviewing, and developing salespeople.

Have fun out there! Hire the right people; listen to your customers; treat your salespeople with dignity; make a lot of money. And again, thanks for buying the book!